D0027891

MONTESSORI TODAY

△ ▽ △

ALSO AVAILABLE FROM SCHOCKEN

Montessori:
A Modern Approach
by Paula Polk Lillard

Dr. Montessori's Own Handbook:
A Short Guide to Her Ideas and Materials
by Maria Montessori

The Montessori Method
by Maria Montessori

MONTESSORI
△ ▽ △ TODAY

A Comprehensive Approach to
Education from Birth to Adulthood

PAULA POLK LILLARD

SCHOCKEN BOOKS
New York

Copyright (c) 1996 by Paula Polk Lillard

All rights reserved under International and Pan-American Copyright Conventions.
Published in the United States by Schocken Books Inc., New York, and simultaneously in Canada by Random House Of Canada Limited, Toronto. Distributed
by Pantheon Books, a division of Random House, Inc., New York.

Photographs copyright © 1996 by Karin Olsen Campia
Charts copyright © 1996 by Denise Selhausen
Grateful acknowledgment is made to Rebecca Makkai for permission to reprint
"A Student's Reflections," copyright © 1996 by Rebecca Makkai. Reprinted by
permission of Rebecca Makkai.

Library of Congress Cataloging-in-Publication Data

Lillard, Paula Polk.
    Montessori today: a comprehensive approach to education from
birth to adulthood / by Paula Polk Lillard.
        p. cm.
    Includes bibliographical references and index.
    ISBN 0-8052-1061-x
    1. Montessori method of education.   2. Education, Elementary.
I. Title.
LB775.M8L55   1996
371.3'92—dc20   95-4608
                                                         CIP

BOOK DESIGN BY LAURA HOUGH
Manufactured in the United States of America

20 19 18 17 16 15

To my mother and father

with gratitude for their heritage

of courage, service,

and zest for life and its lessons

"Whatever an education is, it should make you a unique individual, not a conformist; it should furnish you with an original spirit with which to tackle the big challenges; it should allow you to find values which will be your road map through life; it should make you spiritually rich, a person who loves whatever you are doing, wherever you are, whomever you are with; it should teach you what is important, how to live and how to die."

—From *Dumbing Us Down* by John Taylor Gatto, recipient of a New York State Teacher Award

Contents

Contents

(Photographs follow page 97.)

ACKNOWLEDGMENTS

Margaret Stephenson, Montessori teacher and international trainer from the United Kingdom and United States, has been my inspiration and mentor in writing about Montessori theory and practice for nearly thirty years. I owe her my deepest gratitude, not only for her guidance and encouragement to me personally but for her lifelong dedication to the highest standards in Montessori education worldwide.

I thank all of my Montessori colleagues who responded so generously to requests for clarification on Montessori theory and information on research and growth of Montessori schools today. I am especially grateful to Marsilia Palocci, member of the Pedagogical Committee of the Association Montessori Internationale, for her help with in-depth understanding of Montessori's concept of universal human tendencies.

It has been a joyful experience to engage in the teaching-learning process with the children, parents, and staff of the Forest Bluff School. This book could not have been written without the love and support that we have shared. Laura Earls in particular gave unstintingly of her time and expertise concerning the elementary classroom.

I am very appreciative of the help which Susan Jasper gave in my household and personal affairs in the past months, which made it possible for me to both write and teach.

I was fortunate in having Bonny Fetterman as my editor at Schocken Books. She offered both wise counsel and understanding of the educational vision which I hoped to convey.

To the bulwarks of my daily life—my husband of almost forty-five years, my daughters, sons-in-law, and grandchildren—I owe every debt but especially for their patience, encouragement, and support in the writing of this book.

I have endeavored in my writing to be true to the principles of Maria Montessori and the educational system which she began. I accept sole responsibility for my understanding and explanation of them as expressed in this book.

PREFACE

This book is an overview of Montessori theory and practice, with special emphasis on the child's elementary-school years, for parents, teachers, and all those who are concerned about education today. I felt compelled to write this book. Let me explain why, in part, by relating a recent conversation.

I had been on an airplane, seated next to a man who looked of an age to be the father of young children. As it happened, I learned that he had two sons, ages nine and eleven, both attending a large Montessori school in Chicago since they were three years old. Because this school followed its elementary level with a middle school program, this father was planning for his sons to remain there until age fifteen. They would then go on to public or private school; he was not certain which one and expected that his sons would have a role in making the final choice.

I asked him how he had come to choose a Montessori education for his children. "It was my wife's decision," he said. "I was busy with my work. I left it up to her. In fact, I was not in favor of their staying in Montessori when they reached first grade. I was worried that it was too sheltered an environment. I've changed over the years. I've become very involved."

When I asked what he liked about Montessori, he responded that it was the sense of teamwork that the children developed and their self-direction. "They are competitive," he said. "All kids are, but it is different. They get along so well and they are so confident. They are almost adultlike in their attitudes toward others. They care about the world. They have even gotten me involved in a community-service project for the homeless." He paused then and said, "I realize that I'm not telling you about Montessori. I'm telling you what my children are like because of going to a Montessori school."

He then commented about the other children in the neighborhood who were friends of his sons, many of whom attended a fashionable private school with a reputation for high academic achievement. "I don't mean to bad-mouth these children," he continued. "They are basically good kids but they are pseudosophisticated, even to the point of being smart alecks. I don't get any sense that they care about doing their best for its own sake. Their focus seems to be on beating others."

I asked this father if he was worried about his oldest son's transition to high school, where he would be with these neighborhood children or others like them who had had such a different experience in their early schooling. He answered quickly, "Yes, because I'm afraid that my son will seem eccentric to them. He's always studying something, looking up the answer to some question of his." Immediately, however, he reversed himself. "Actually, no. I don't think it will be a problem because he is so confident. He won't be bothered by teasing if it comes to that.

He gets along with everyone and he is used to being independent. It's a fear that I have."

He went on to describe his own early education. He had gone to both public elementary and high school in a district which I recognized as one of the best in the Chicago suburbs. Yet, he said that it had been a lonely experience. "None of my teachers were mentors to me. It was all so cold. Montessori is such a caring way to teach," he continued.

Eventually, I explained my work in Montessori education. "In that case, let me ask you a question about something that bothers me," he responded. "Not everyone knows about Montessori. Why not? It's so good."

I understood his frustration. Indeed, forty years have passed since I began teaching second grade in the public school of Terrace Park, Ohio, and still our schools are no closer in connecting the education of children to their development as human beings: each child as an individual with a unique contribution to make to the world. Until this is done, our schools will fail to help children become active learners, connected to their society, and empowered to accomplish things within it.

Parents look to schools to help prepare their children for the world of change in which we live. Unfortunately, they consistently find educational systems geared to the past, built upon rewards and punishments, grading curves and class rank, rote memorization and testing. Primarily sitting and listening, each student is isolated at a desk with little opportunity for developing the social and communicative skills required for solving problems in the real world.

In addition, in the last decade, standards of behavior and discipline in schools have steadily declined. Defiance, rudeness, and varying degrees of violence are increasingly commonplace among students. Parents are concerned about the impact of a negative school atmosphere on the values and attitudes of their children.

Periodically, attempts at educational reform have been tried. In the 1960s, one approach, that of the open classroom, followed the publication of John Holt's classic book, *How Children Fail.* This approach freed the classroom teacher from the lockstep methods of the regular school curriculum, allowing for more attention to the needs of individual students and creating a more relaxed and joyful learning environment. This reform movement and others like it did not, however, contain well-defined academic components capable of helping children to meet high standards in literacy, mathematics, and the abilities to think and communicate clearly; nor did they understand the necessity of viewing the child's education in its entirety. Goals and methods at each age level must form a cohesive whole if children are to reach their full potential for individual development. These reform efforts were, therefore, doomed ultimately to fail.

In the early 1960s, I became aware of an approach to education that balances freedom with responsibility in the classroom and also sets high standards of intellectual and social development for children. Equally important, it encompasses a vision of the development of human beings from childhood to early adulthood. As a result, it is a logical and consistent plan of education that follows the child from one developmental stage to the next. This unique educational approach is the Montessori method.

I was fortunate to have my first exposure to Montessori education in the classroom. I came to this experience without preconceived ideas and saw for myself the benefits for the children. I was an assistant in a preschool classroom which the third of my then four children attended. It gradually became clear to me during that first year that the Montessori approach is firmly rooted in the developmental patterns of children. It appeared to be this grounding in stages of development, as well as its freeing up of natural human energy and appeal to intrinsic motivation, which led to the children's heightened intellectual and social achievement. In this classroom, the indirect preparation (in both language and numeration) begun when they were three years old, made it possible for five-year-old children to begin to read and write spontaneously and to complete mathematical problems in addition, subtraction, multiplication, and division with an understanding of the decimal system. They reached this unusual level of development through a process of exploration and discovery with concrete, hands-on materials.

Just as important, in terms of human development, these children were independent and confident in the classroom, and their creativity, happiness, and love of learning were evident. I remember being particularly surprised by the children's unusual kindness and concern for each other and the care with which they handled the objects of their environment. In fact, I had never seen children so young behave with the same degree of self-discipline and responsibility.

In the following years I completed a Master's degree in education at Xavier University in Cincinnati, Ohio, and volunteered for Montessori community projects including several Head Start programs and a Montessori research study at the University of Cincinnati. At the end of this period, I wrote a book, *Montessori: A Modern Approach*, to serve as an introduction to Montessori education for parents of preschool children.

It was not until 1981 that I became a Montessori teacher, certified by the Association Montessori Internationale.[1] In that year, I took the international training course for the primary level at the Milwaukee Montessori Institute. At the same time, I fulfilled my dream of beginning my own Montessori elementary school. With the second of my five grown children, Lynn Jessen, an experienced Montessori teacher and Jane Linari, a friend and teaching colleague, I cofounded the Forest Bluff School in Lake Bluff, Illinois.

Lynn taught the first class of fifteen three- and four-year-old children. The following year this preschool classroom comprised twenty-five children, and Jane started an elementary class. The school has since expanded and now has approximately one hundred and fifty children ages eighteen months to fifteen years. The children come from communities in the Chicago area, some of them commuting for as long as one hour. We have nine Montessori teachers and eight classroom assistants, as well as a business manager and secretary. Each teacher shares in the administrative duties of the school. This shared responsibility has enabled us to build a strong sense of teamwork and has eliminated the bureaucratic structures burdening many schools today. It has also allowed us to make administrative decisions with an educational focus, thus keeping the combined needs of child, parent, and teacher foremost.

I have taught one of the primary classrooms for three-to-six-year-olds for the past ten years. It is an experience that, next to marriage and motherhood, I treasure above all else in my life. Sitting on the floor, studying the new puzzle map of Asia, learning to pronounce the names of Kazakhstan, Azerbaijan, Kyrgyzstan, and Tajikistan along with the children—who do so much more readily than I do—I am caught up in the children's enthusiasm for discovering their world.

△ △ △

This book conveys the breadth of the Montessori approach in helping children develop as integrated adults. It demonstrates how Montessori education combines freedom with responsibility, a more active role for the children in their own learning, high standards of academic excellence, social awareness and moral development, and a vision of humanity and its accomplishments that inspires children to take their place in their communities, when the time comes, as responsible, contributing adults.

The success of Montessori education is based on the understanding that, from the beginning, the child's education must be viewed in its entirety. Goals and methods at each age level must fit together to form a cohesive whole, from birth to adulthood. The following chapters present the Montessori approach as a consistent plan of education that follows the child from one developmental stage of self-formation to the next, recognizing that each plane of development must build upon the last. The role of education at each age level is to aid this process of ongoing development for each child.

Chapter 1 presents a brief introduction to the origin and theory of Montessori education. Parents primarily interested in the practical aspects of the day-to-day classroom may want to go directly to later chapters, referring back to this foundation chapter whenever they need background information. Chapter 2 gives an overview of Montessori education at the primary level. I have not repeated here the more extensive information on children under six years old which is covered in my book, *Montessori: A Modern Approach*. Those readers wishing further details on the education of the younger child, whether at home or at school, should refer to this earlier work. The main body of this present book, representing the child's elementary years, consists of Chapters 3 through 8. To my knowledge, this is the first time that Montessori theory and practice for the elementary classroom is presented in detail for the lay person. Chapter 9 briefly describes Montessori's ideas for high-school and university education. It is intended to help parents visualize where their children will be at the end of their Montessori elementary education and to anticipate needs as children move into adolescence and early adulthood. Chapter 9 encompasses the whole of Montessori's educational vision, for it relates the young person's strengths and goals during the critical years of emerging adulthood.

The final chapter describes the status of Montessori education in the United States today, and its potential contribution for the future. I outline the role of charter and magnet schools in the spread of Montessori elementary education in public schools, as well as the growth of independent Montessori schools. I also discuss the present state of research in Montessori education and the preparation of Montessori students for their further education.

Montessori designed her plan for the elementary classroom based upon the Montessori child's advanced state of self-formation made possible by Montessori education in the first six years of life. Parents therefore may be concerned that their children cannot benefit from a Montessori elementary education if they have not been able first to attend a Montessori primary school. Fortunately, this is not the case. Montessori teachers, like all good teachers everywhere, take children where they find them and use whatever means necessary to help them in their development. In fact, Montessori elementary teachers have an advantage in this regard because of the flexibility and individual approach built into Montessori education at every age level. Some of the most successfully developing elementary students and graduates of our school did not attend our primary program.

On the other hand, the advantages to children who have attended a primary Montessori classroom before going on to the elementary level will become obvious to the reader in the chapters of this book outlining the elementary program. These "prepared" children are accustomed to accepting responsibility for their actions within a community of others and to initiating and completing work independent of constant teacher direction. They are ready to explore and discover with the Montessori materials and to complete written and oral research projects with their companions from their first day in the elementary classroom. If other children do not know how to read, write, and compute, they must spend their beginning months learning how to do so. These children's capacity for self-direction and living responsibly with others may also require special help, depending upon their previous experiences both at home and in play groups, day-care or other preschool programs.

A word of caution: The name "Montessori" is in the public domain. It may be used anywhere by anyone for any purpose. Therefore, "Montessori" has become attached to programs to which it may be applicable only to a limited degree, or perhaps not at all. Therefore, it is important that parents observe classrooms in the school which they are considering to determine whether this school meets the standards of an authentic Montessori school.

As new discoveries are made about human development,

particularly through modern neurological studies, additions and changes in Montessori education may well occur. No one person can find all the answers to any problem, let alone one as complex as aiding human development in its formative years. I have described here the Montessori classrooms and practices of which I have been a part. They represent a time and a place in history. To the extent that they are based on universal principles of human development, they will apply to all historical circumstances. To the extent that they are found not to be so based, they will not endure. With this understanding in mind, I hope to explain in this book the advantages of Montessori education as I have known them—as a parent, as a teacher, and as a grandparent.

MONTESSORI TODAY

△ ▽ △

1

△ △ △

THE ORIGIN AND THEORY OF MONTESSORI EDUCATION

Maria Montessori concentrated upon the goal of education, rather than its methods. She defined this goal as "the development of a complete human being, oriented to the environment, and adapted to his or her time, place and culture." This adaptation involves the capacity to meet new situations and to have the intelligence and courage to transform them when change is needed. Today we might define this goal as the preparation of children to live successfully in *their* world, by which we mean the future, rather than to live primarily in ours, which is the present and the past.

Montessori had no preconceived ideas as to how to reach this goal for children. Her approach was to focus on the children and to observe their needs. She believed that within the formative years of children lay the answers to humanity's ability to renew itself in each succeeding generation. Montessori was both a pragmatist and a visionary. She was a pragmatist in that she gathered evidence in an objective and unprejudiced manner directly from children in their natural settings. She was a visionary in her faith that the answers which she sought would lead not only to more meaningful lives for individual children but would contribute to humanity itself.

Montessori, a medical doctor and pioneer educator, was born in Italy in 1870 and died in 1952. She lived principally in Italy, Spain, India, and the Netherlands through a turbulent period of World Wars and revolutions. Although uprooted many times in her life and several times a refugee, she continued to study children, establish schools, give lectures, and train teachers on three continents. Today there are Montessori schools in fifty-two countries on six continents, and their number continues to expand worldwide.

Montessori based her educational plan upon the observation of children in diverse cultures and in many countries. Therefore, her discoveries are not accurately described as Montessori principles. They are universal principles of human behavior, which belong to all peoples, societies, and cultures. These universal principles are a sound foundation for educational systems everywhere.

Montessori considered her work as ongoing. Therefore, she did not attempt to formulate her ideas into a final theory of education. However, in her last three years of life, when she was already in her eighties, she looked back upon her life's work and presented the essence of her ideas in an overview. Three main theses appear in this summary:

> that human development does not occur in a steady, linear ascent but in a series of formative planes
>
> that the complete development of human beings is made possible by their tendencies to certain universal actions in relation to their environment

that this interaction with the environment is most productive in terms of the individual's development when it is self-chosen and founded upon individual interest.

As a young medical student at the University of Rome in the 1890s, Montessori studied the origin and formation of living beings. When she returned to the University of Rome, after a successful medical career, to study pedagogy, philosophy, and anthropology, Montessori continued to be intrigued by development in all forms of life. As she worked with children and young adults in the following years, she gradually recognized that there were specific stages in human formation. Eventually, she identified four such planes of development. There are two planes of childhood, resulting at age twelve in a mature child and two formative stages of adulthood, completed when a young adult reaches maturity at age twenty-four.

These four planes of development form the structural outline of this book. The details specific to each plane are covered in the pertinent chapters. In this introductory chapter, however, I discuss those principles and general information that are germane to all four planes.

Montessori discovered that three things are happening in each of the four formative planes:

there is a specific goal in development

there is a readily identified direction being followed to reach that goal

there are specific sensitivities given to human beings in each period of development which facilitate reaching the definitive goal for that plane.

To highlight the dramatic nature of the child's transitions from one plateau of development to the next, Montessori likened developmental planes to the metamorphoses of a butterfly. The various stages of larva, chrysalis, and adult butterfly are so radically different as to be unrecognizable one from the other. So, too, the differences of each plane of human formation are so extraordinary that the young person appears in each as a re-created being. Each of these four planes of development builds upon the last so that faulty development in any one affects the successful completion of all the others.

Montessori observed that regular education takes no heed of these planes of development. In virtually every country in the world, the first stage of development, from birth to age six, is ignored because schooling does not begin until it is over or nearly so. Beginning at the child's sixth year, education follows a steady ascent, becoming increasingly more difficult each year with more and more subjects added, more and more teachers introduced, more and more study and production required, based on outwardly imposed curriculum and tests.

In spite of being a successful student in such a system herself, winning many prizes and honors throughout her schooling and university courses, Montessori saw many errors in this approach. She referred to the school children of her day as so many "dried butterflies" pinned to a display board. She drew a chart depicting the linear ascent of education based as it is upon feeding information to children as if they are blanks to be imprinted upon. She colored it in an "awful greyness" to reflect the boredom it inflicted on the children. Its underlying assumption is that intelligence increases with age.

In contrast Montessori drew a chart reflecting the actual de-

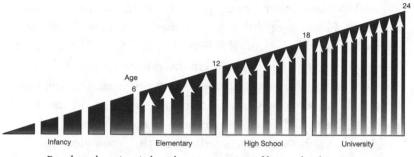

*Regular education is based on assumption of linear development
(arrows represent increasing pressure).*

velopment of children. It shows that in each plane there is an emergence or rebirth of development that reaches a peak and then declines. It emphasizes the uniformity and regularity of human development in this regard.

Montessori believed that schooling should correspond to the child's developmental periods. "Instead of dividing schools into nursery, primary, secondary, and university, we should divide education in planes and each of these should correspond to the phase the developing individual goes through."[1]

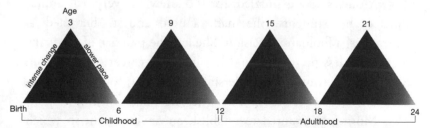

Montessori education is geared to peaks and valleys of human formation.

Montessori became aware that regular education is not sufficient to the needs of children. As a medical doctor, she was responsible for the care of children in the State Orthophrenic School in Rome. Uneducable children were gathered in this school from other institutions of the city: orphanages, asylums, hospitals, and schools. Montessori was interested in the development of these children as human beings, rather than as "school children." As she was concerned about their complete health, both physical and spiritual, she began to try to reach their minds, and especially as their minds related to the control of their bodies in behavior.

Montessori studied the pioneer work of everyone that she could find who had contributed to this field. Throughout her life, she acknowledged her supreme debt to two earlier French physicians, Jean Itard and Edouard Séguin, who had developed methods for helping both mentally deficient and deaf children. Montessori devised various materials of her own, as well as using those of Itard and Séguin, to help her children. To everyone's astonishment many of these children not only learned to read and write but, in state examinations at least, equaled their peers of the regular school system. This was the same system that had earlier rejected them as "uneducable."

Montessori was puzzled, for she knew the very real limitations of her students. She made a bold and, to her medical colleagues, a foolhardy decision. She left the practice of medicine for the far less prestigious and less lucrative career of education. She was determined to understand how she could have succeeded where her children's former teachers had failed.

Montessori wanted to establish an environment in which school-age children of normal ability could be observed using her new materials and methods. In particular, she resolved not to be prejudiced by past educational approaches, nor to disturb the natural behavior of the children in her new classroom environment with a schedule of demands and interruptions for this or that required activity.

As it happened, she had no opportunity to work with school-age children, as they were already attending public schools. However, an occasion arose to have custody, for most of the day, of children below school age. These children lived in a reclaimed public-housing project in one of Rome's most disreputable sections: the San Lorenzo district.

It was by accident and not by design, then, that Montessori first tried her ideas and new materials with preschool children. Because the children of San Lorenzo reacted even more positively to her educational environment and its subsequent revisions than the children of the State Orthophrenic School, Montessori determined that the customary schooling needed not mere reform; education needed a revolution. This revolution must include a recognition of the developmental stages of human formation and a realization of the goals, directions, and powers or characteristics pertinent to each. It must go further. Montessori proposed that this revolution in education be built upon the basic responses of human beings which make possible their complete development and adaptation to their environment. She believed that she was successful with the children in Rome and San Lorenzo, and subsequently children throughout Europe, because she had inadvertently developed an educational plan that did precisely this.

Tendencies to positive interaction with the environment belong to human beings of all ages. However, they do not operate in the same way throughout life. They take a different direction at each plane of development and, again, in mature life. They are equally important to successful education in every period of life whether in childhood, beginning adulthood, maturity, or old age. Montessori did not identify human tendencies to certain behaviors and seek to develop an educational plan based upon them. It happened the other way round. She observed children and then responded to their behavior.

Whenever Montessori stood back to reflect on her work with children, she was driven more by questions than answers. By the mid-1940s, she could see that her prepared environments for children from birth through age twelve were assisting their development in positive ways. But why? What made the children respond as they did? Why did they not just stand there in the doorway? What made them eager to enter Montessori environments and to use the materials within them for their self-formation? What gave the children their power and their energy?

Whatever is supplying this ability to respond to the environment has belonged to all human beings, child or adult, male or female, from the beginning. It, therefore, represents a universal principle of human behavior. When such principles are allowed to operate, the power of human beings for a positive response to life is released. When they are thwarted, people of all ages are correspondingly crippled.

Both as an educator and as an anthropologist, Montessori reflected upon the natural behavior of human beings in relation to their environment. When she returned to the University of Rome to engage in further studies, she subsequently became a Professor of Anthropology and remained in that post for a number of years. She was familiar with primitive human societies and their responses to varied environments. With this background, it was natural for Montessori to look back to early humans on earth, to reflect on their behaviors in response to their as yet not understood environment and to look for similarities with the behavior of human beings today, particularly children who also must discover a world unknown to them.

Montessori recognized that human beings do not possess instincts to allow them to meet their needs and ensure their survival, as animals do. Instead, human beings have tendencies toward certain behaviors that help them fulfill their needs—primary needs for food, shelter, and clothing; and secondary ones for defense and transportation. Montessori identified these behaviors for the purposes of discussion. It was not her intention to create a comprehensive list of the ways all people interact with the environment, nor to specify terminology for describing that behavior. She used different definitions of behavioral tendencies on separate occasions, reflecting her primary role as an educational practitioner rather than a psychological theorist. The following terms, however, can be considered representative of those which she mentioned at various times in her training lectures. They are: *exploration, orientation, order, imagination, manipulation, repetition, precision, control of error leading to perfection,* and *communication*. Montessori classrooms work well when the teacher understands the necessity of continually appealing to children's innate behaviors that lead to their adaptation to society and, ultimately, the possibility of changing that society.

Montessori noted that from the beginning it was the relationship of human intelligence to tendencies toward certain behaviors that made it possible for human beings to discover reality, thus allowing them to use every environment from the desert to the arctic in meeting their needs for survival. The first human beings appear to have been very limited in their intelligence. We speculate on the basis of the few skulls found by archaeologists. Even if their intelligence was only a spark above the animals, however, early humans set out to explore the unknown as free agents, unrestricted by instincts. They could choose either ants or newly killed animals for their food, shelters made of brush or caves, animal skins or grasses for their clothing.

Children, who must discover their environment, face a similar challenge to that of early humans. Children differ, however, in that they have, as yet, incomplete and unformed bodies for this exploration. This apparent weakness is, in fact, an advantage, because it gives children the ability to adapt to the time and place in which each one is born. Human tendencies to certain behaviors then are the means by which the child becomes a part of a specific human group. In addition, behavioral tendencies of human beings have a relationship to human freedom. Children not only can become a part of a specific human group; as they mature, their behavioral tendencies make it possible for them to change that group.

Because human tendencies are basic to an understanding of Montessori education and because their fundamental role in aiding children in their development is seldom recognized by parents and teachers, I will expand briefly on their individual manifestations in children and adults, as noted by Montessori.

Montessori regarded exploration as a fundamental behavior of human beings from their beginnings. The first human beings had to search their unknown surrounding environment in order to find the sources for meeting their primary needs. Exploration then was the predominant force in human activity from the earliest days, bringing with it, when successful, the exhilaration of achievement. Even today when we set out to explore the challenge of the unknown, the joy of pre-historic human beings still comes to us.

Children begin their exploration of the earth's environment from the first moment after birth. They are immediately bombarded with light, sound, smell, and touch of skin. Montessori described this initial experience of the child as a "second birth" because it represents the beginning of a second embryological life—this time outside the womb. Even if they appear to be doing nothing, motionless infants are exploring in their cribs. It is an invisible exploration of hearing, looking, and feeling air and touch upon the skin. These impressions are so fundamental that they shape the development of the child's brain. Within the first fifteen days after birth, an entire neurological network has formed. The infant, as explorer, has "gone out" into the environment, taken it in and come back a different individual, just as all explorers search and find knowledge and bring it back for their use.

The human need to know enables the child to finish his or her own body and brain and to become a human being of the time and place where he or she is born. The child's goal then in exploration is twofold: to finish his or her own body through the development of the brain via exploration of the environment and to adapt to the group in which he or she is born. The great pull toward this twofold goal is implicit in Montessori's conception of human tendencies. One usage of the Italian word, *tendere*, relates to the archer's pulling of the cord of a bow with an arrow aimed directly at its target. This image of power and singleness of purpose, as represented by the pulled bow and poised arrow, gives a clear indication of the driving force which Montessori attributes to human tendencies in directing human behavior.

As we shall see, Montessori education at each succeeding

level is predicated upon the basic human urge to explore. The environments for children under six years old offer a feast of exploration for children, not of a fantasy world as in many preschools and day-care centers but the world of reality that the first human beings set out to explore. The elementary program, secondary level, and plan for the university continue this exploration of the real world, extending it beyond the classroom into the community and, eventually, to the world at large.

As those first human beings explored farther and farther from their point of origin, they had to have some means for returning to their starting place. Only in this way could they have achieved the freedom and independence to move about. We must then have a tendency to put ourselves in relation to our environment, to make a pattern of it in our minds. We have to be able to review this mental map: to make an order of it in our minds. We have to know where to start, where to go next, and where to finish. In order for the first human beings to find their way in their explorations, orientation and order had to have been tendencies of their behavior.

The moment that the child receives impressions, he or she must hold them within the brain in an accessible pattern. There is, then, a tendency to order these impressions within the mind for future use. This personal classification of impressions is limited, however, if it does not coincide with those relationships that the culture accepts. Montessori devised materials that assist the child in understanding this broader classification of impressions. By their means, the child is given access to the scientific world. Sensorial materials assist the child in establishing an understanding of comparative relationships in size, weight, length, and volume, for example. This is not the first time that the child handles objects of different size or weight. It is the extension of dealing with the relationships among objects, however, that is important for cultural adaptation. Thus the child learns to distinguish: heavy, heavier, heaviest or thin, thinner, thinnest. The child becomes a member of his or her society, possessing the key to interacting with all its scientific knowledge. From a cognitive point of view, exploration is no longer purely sensorial but is extended to a higher level.

Order and orientation are facilitated in the Montessori classroom by a well-structured environment, the sequencing of materials, and the consistency of educational approach. Each material has its own place in the room where it can always be found when it is not in use. This outward order is dependent upon an internal one related to the practical development of moral standards. In a communal situation, for example, we put objects for use back in the place and condition we found them out of respect for others. Lectures about such behavior are of little use to human beings; these are experiences we must live at an early age.

The children are introduced to the materials in a Montessori environment in an orderly sequence and logical progression. Sequence of materials gives the children an experience of orientation in cause and effect. Eighteen-month-olds learn that, when washing, they wet their hands first, then use soap, rinse, and dry with the towel and not the other way around. From logical progression in their activities, they develop their capacity for logical and orderly thought. Enhancement of the children's natural tendencies to order and orientation in the Montessori environment enables them to feel great confidence there. This is a place that they can manage and, therefore, they feel safe. This sense of security is not just the result of having a loving teacher upon whom they can depend; it is the natural outcome of the children being in a place where they can trust their own powers. It is psychological security, engendered in part by a properly structured environment, which gives children the impulse to try harder to face the unknown, including the unpleasant facts of life. The goal is to help children use their human energies to deal with the failures and disappointments of their lives and not to be destroyed by them.

To meet their needs for survival, the first human beings must have had tendencies beyond exploration, orientation, and order. They must have had the ability to imagine and to create abstractions. Hence, early humans could observe the horns of an animal and imagine sharp instruments for their own defense, see the bird's nest and imagine the construction of a shelter, notice the animal's fur and realize that it could be used to keep them warm.

Imagining solutions, however, would not have been sufficient for survival. Human beings had to have a means for carrying out these solutions. This outcome was achieved by combining intelligence and the capacity for manipulation by the hand with the powers of imagination and abstraction. Human intelligence and imagination could create an image in the mind; the hand could bring this imaginative thought into relation with the concrete world. Hence, earlier human beings could see that the chair with two legs would not stand, the wheel improperly fashioned would not go round smoothly. Through continuing manipulation and changing of these objects, the hand could report to the intelligence where it was in error. The process of thinking could then become clear through a circular procedure from the mind to the hand to control of what the mind had created and back to the mind. This feedback loop from thinking to repeated manipulation and control of error makes possible the human search for precision and perfection.

Human tendencies of imagination and abstraction, manipulation and repetition are, therefore, interdependent with the remaining human propensities for precision, control of error, and perfection. Through these behavioral tendencies, human beings have managed to create a supernature: imagining solutions to human needs, trying them out and, if successful, using them to help in survival.

When young children are engaged in this circular process from abstraction to manipulation, repetition and control of error in their striving for precision and perfection in Montessori classrooms, there is both an earnestness and a peace about their activity. The pleasure that the children are experiencing is evident; but its outer manifestations are muted. Sometimes a young child will exclaim, "I did it!" in a triumphant tone. More often the reaction is a light in the eyes or a quiet smile and perhaps the soft-spoken words, "I did it again." This calmer reaction of the young child in discovery is sometimes misunderstood by adults when they visit Montessori classrooms. We are accustomed to seeing children in settings that do not foster this deeper reaction to the environment. It is important to understand that the joy that comes to children in this all-inclusive exploration is intense, although the children's outward appearance is one of seriousness and concentrated effort.

One last behavioral tendency is equally important with those already mentioned to maintain the quality and continued progression of human life. It is the propensity to develop communication by means of language. It is through communication that human beings have cooperated with each other to solve common problems, and it is through communication based on written and oral language in particular that each generation has passed on its accumulated wisdom to the next.

The development of language is a mysterious phenomenon. The child takes in the image of a tree and from many such images of trees the concept "tree" is gradually formed. The idea of a tree is as real in the child's mind as the tree itself is in the real world. The child can carry this idea, "tree," in the mind and have it available for use in any circumstance. There is still a higher level of awareness that the child must reach. The tree is only a concept in the child's mind. It needs now to be expressed in reality through sound and symbol. When human beings accomplish this, they can give the gift of their own minds to others. Einstein developed the idea of relativity. It had an existence within his mind. It was as real to him as the idea of a tree might be to others. He then had to search for symbols to communicate this complex reality of his own making to others. By doing this, he made a contribution to all humanity.[2] The desire to communicate our ideas to others can be considered as part of the spiritual makeup of human beings, for through this process we give our discoveries willingly to others including unborn generations.

As we shall see, the children's development of language and communication of thought is unique in Montessori classrooms. From the time that they come in the morning, the children never stop talking to each other for long. This occurs because the teacher is freed from the role of lecturing from the front of the classroom, driving, and controlling the educational process. The compelling force of human communication is dramatically evident in the Children's House, as the Montessori primary school is called, when the moment comes that five-year-olds explode into writing. This past year it occurred in the spring. The children were everywhere, writing and illustrating their stories, and copying the text and drawing the pictures from the small books that they were now beginning to read voluntarily to themselves and to each other. It brought an excitement to the room that everyone felt, the younger children as well as the older ones. Three-year-olds put their rugs close to the older children to do their work, as if this new "magic" might rub off on them. Four-year-olds redoubled their efforts with the Movable Alphabets and chalkboards, as if sensing that this was the route to these exciting new achievements. When the children arrive in the elementary classroom, they have already achieved an advanced level of oral and written communication. Now it is their freedom to communicate and work together in small self-formed groups that is everywhere apparent. As we will discover in a later chapter describing an elementary classroom in process, it is the sharing of ideas and books that provides the spontaneity and momentum of Montessori elementary education.

These human behavioral tendencies described by Montessori—exploration, orientation, order, imagination, manipulation, repetition, precision, control of error and perfection, and communication—are present throughout life, although they do not operate uniformly in the formative stages, the years from birth to twenty-four. Exploration for a two-year-old is a different matter from that of a ten-year-old or a sixteen-year-old. This realization substantiates Montessori's argument for new divisions in education based upon the child's developmental stages and requiring different educational environments for each.

We have now discussed the first two of Montessori's theses related to her educational ideas: the development of the child through specific planes of formation and human tendencies to certain behaviors which have guaranteed the survival of human beings and given them not only the possibility of adaptation to any group but the ability to effect changes in those groups as well. Montessori's final concept concerning education involves the child's activity based upon a self-chosen interest. This principle is predicated upon the first two: interest is founded in the stage of formation the young person is experiencing, as well as in the personal interests of each individual. Activity is derived from behavioral urges in response to the environment. Activity is therefore universal while interest is both universal, according to the plane of formation, and specific, in relation to a unique personality.

This last principle of human development reveals another fallacy in the customary approach to education. Human beings do not develop meaningful knowledge by force. We may be coerced into memorizing abstract information, but it is soon forgotten. Rather, it is the human tendencies to manipulate our environment that lead us to build a strong conceptual base for further knowledge and hence to retain it.

Modern technology shows us that our brains are physiologically changed in this process of interacting with our environment. As our brains develop, we can manipulate ever more abstract concepts, but their basis remains in our original sensorial impressions of the material world. Children must form these sensorial impressions through their own activity. The adult cannot do this for them. Equally important, children cannot do this for themselves if they are forced to sit in a chair and only watch or listen to others. They must *act* for themselves.

We know that Montessori did not set out with any ambition to design a plan of education to correspond with principles of human behavior. Perhaps this was the inevitable result, however. She was, after all, watching children and observing what they did when allowed to follow their own inclinations. Which actions inspired them to further positive activity? What gave them observable satisfaction and thus inspired ever deeper involvement? Conversely, what actions resulted in negative behavior and a deterioration in concentration and meaningful effort?

The educational plan that Montessori eventually evolved, based upon her observations and which we will discuss in detail in later chapters, contains three essential elements: a prepared environment, a prepared adult, and freedom with responsibility. By changing the details of fulfillment for each of these criteria in the differing planes of development, Montessori allowed for the changing needs and interests of the child in successive ages. Far from being a continuous linear ascent as in regular education, Montessori education alters with each plane in the child's development. In this way, each stage serves as a solid foundation upon which the next may be built.

Despite the differing directions of the components in Montessori education at each plane, their principles remain the same. The prepared environment is always a place of simplicity, beauty, and order. There is nothing within it that could be an obstacle to the children's development. This means the environment is uncluttered and conducive to activity and concentration.

Much has been made of the educational materials that Montessori placed in her environments for children under six and from six through twelve years old. Montessori and her many colleagues designed these materials over the years, and they are continuously reviewed and revised by the Association Montessori

Internationale. These materials are indeed impressive both in design and quality.

Because they are beautifully executed and highly visible, many people make the mistake of equating the whole of Montessori education with these specially designed materials. In fact, the materials are secondary. It is the totality of the prepared environment to be explored and acted upon by the children that is primary: the other children, the teacher, the nonmanufactured Montessori materials, and the careful arrangement of the classroom. It is possible to have an environment that meets the essentials of Montessori education when no manufactured Montessori materials are available. Conversely, not every classroom with a full complement of manufactured materials meets all the criteria of a quality Montessori environment.

The prepared adult acts as a link to the environment for the child. Montessori teachers do not "teach" the child in the usual sense. They observe the children in order to discover their needs and interests based on their stages in self-formation and their individual personalities. They then attempt to present just the materials or activities to the children that match their developmental needs. It is in the children's subsequent independent use of these materials and activities that learning takes place.

In the end, it is freedom that allows the children's self-formation. Montessori called freedom "the key to the process of development." When she first discussed freedom in relation to children at the beginning of the twentieth century, no one knew what she was talking about. Children were to be seen and not heard. Today, parents embrace the idea of freedom for their children. However, Montessori's idea of freedom is not always understood by parents. Freedom does not mean doing whatever we want, particularly if we are children. Children are in a process of self-formation. Allowing children to do whatever they wish is condemning them to the mercy of their whims and desires of the moment. These will often be destructive to themselves, to others, and to their environment.

In reality, to be free means to be in control of self, to be able to do what one chooses to do, not what one's feelings or illogical thoughts of the moment may dictate. In order for children to build such self-discipline, adults must be firm, fair, and consistent in setting limits from the child's earliest years onward. A parent may decide that her very young child may choose between apples or oranges for lunch; but the child is not free to eat nothing. Children may help to set the table or do the dishes; they are not free not to help with dinner. In the primary classroom children may use the red rods or bake biscuits; they are not free to disturb a child who is busily working. In the elementary classroom, the children may choose their topics of research and their working companions. They are not free to waste their days in aimless activity or idle conversation with their friends.

When Montessori discussed freedom, she invariably mentioned its relationship to responsibility and self-discipline. We need freedom to exercise responsibility; we need the ability to be responsible before we can be truly free. It is essential to the success of Montessori education that adults, whether parents in the home or teachers in the classroom, be self-disciplined and responsible themselves. It is through their example that children discover what it means to live in freedom.

2

△ △ △

OVERVIEW OF THE
PRIMARY YEARS

The first plane in the child's development is from birth to age six. Based on her observations of children, Montessori determined that the overriding goal of this period is the development of the self as an individual being. This goal gives the child an egocentric focus. Adults tend to see this self-centered focus of young children as negative and selfish and attempt to pressure them away from it. This results from judging the child as we would an adult. From the child's point of view, self-centeredness is practical. The infant is born in an unfinished state. There is a monumental task of brain development and self-formation ahead: physical awareness and coordination, will, independence, and language.

Nature is logical. Social life is composed of individuals joining together in groups, nations, and families of nations. Any group is only as strong as its individual members. Development as an individual with specific skills and capacities precedes all other priorities for the infant, so that he or she will have something to contribute to the group when the time comes.

The child's activity to fulfill the goal of development as an individual is a sensorial exploration of fact. The infant touches, tastes, smells, hears, and sees the concrete world. Human tendencies of behavior urge young children to this exploration. They manipulate their immediate environment and repeat their interaction with it until some degree of success is reached.

Montessori observed two special powers that appear to aid children in their task of development as individuals in the first plane: children appear to go through periods of concentrating on specific capacities, and their minds seem to operate differently from ours. She referred to the time frames involved in the child's development of a definitive ability as Sensitive Periods. These are transitory time periods in which the child appears to be working on one specific area of development to the exclusion of all others. Tremendous power and interest are concentrated on one capacity, as if a powerful searchlight focused all its energy on one object for illumination. Sensitive Periods can end abruptly, just as if the same searchlight were suddenly turned off. When a Sensitive Period is passed, it is over forever.

Scientific studies have revealed similar critical periods in development in young animals. However, there is a major difference. Stages in animal development seem to be guided by instinct; the sensitive periods of human childhood represent an intellectual response to the environment. The child not only experiences Sensitive Periods for walking and talking but for the mental attributes of the discovery of order in the environment, attention to precision, interest in minute objects, counting objects, and so forth.

Surprisingly, after the intensity of activity inspired in a Sensitive Period, children do not appear fatigued. Rather, they seem satisfied, calmer, even rested. Montessori believed this was because, by means of this "work" upon the environment, children were actually "creating themselves": that is, their own minds and personalities within the framework of their genetics and biology.[1] Until recently this "creating" of self seemed a fuzzy and unscientific concept. Today technological breakthroughs in viewing the living brain in action make such a concept of self-formation feasible. The child changes the physiology of the brain through interaction with the environment at specific stages of development.[2]

The second observation of Montessori regarding the infant's powers for self-development appeared equally radical when she originally proposed it. Montessori noticed that the infant seems to possess a capacity for absorbing the surrounding environment merely by being in it. Infants stare, hear, smell, and touch; the impressions gained are seemingly incorporated within their minds. This incarnating of impressions is an indiscriminatory act. The child soaks in like a sponge whatever is there: good or bad, beautiful or ugly, peaceful or violent. Montessori surmised that this process is "a natural creative function" of mental development and lays the groundwork for the later emergence of a higher order of thought. Somehow in the process of absorbing images, the child passes "from nothing to a beginning. He or she is bringing into being that most precious gift which gives human beings their superiority—their reason."[3]

There are two stages in this mental absorption of the environment. Montessori called the stage of birth through age three the period of the "unconscious Absorbent Mind." Sensorial impressions are merely registered within the mind. In the second phase, from age three to six, Montessori believed that the child uses these impressions again but, this time, in order to classify and categorize them. Shades of blue now become blue, bluer, bluest, and so forth. She wrote, "The multitudinous impressions unconsciously absorbed, are used again by being known in a different way as the basis on which conscious life is built up. These primordial unconscious impressions are then the stuff out of which is woven consciousness itself, with all that it implies of reason, memory, will and self-knowledge."[4]

In all this process, it is the hand operating with the brain that creates the child's intellect. Montessori called the hand "the instrument of the intelligence." One of the educational tenets of Montessori education is that we should never give to the brain more than we give to the hand; they compose a "twofold creative activity." It is in the children's sixth year that all of their mental work of the hand and brain, working in unison and empowered by the Sensitive Periods and Absorbent Mind, come together in a full integration of personality. The period for sensorial exploration of fact is now complete. The need for focus on individual capacities of movement, will, independence, and language is over.

Montessori's explanation of the child's mental development in the first six years of life sounds esoteric to us today, even though we now know much more about brain development from conception onward. When Montessori first offered her ideas in the early part of the twentieth century, they aroused consternation, even derision. In 1972, I discussed the need for scientific proof of Montessori's observations of the child's mental powers with child development experts. I mentioned my conviction that such proof would be forthcoming in the field of neuroscience, rather than cognitive psychology. It now appears that techniques of brain imagery may make possible such investigative research in the not too distant future.

Since Montessori believed, based upon her observations, that children form themselves in relation to their environment, it was natural for her to regard education as beginning at birth. However, it is important to realize that by education Montessori did not mean an attempt by adults to force the intellectual development of children. Such an approach is foreign to every thought expressed by her. She believed in a "natural unfolding of the child's intelligence." This natural unfolding follows a specific path. It must be aided by the adult, but always as a result of observing the child and following the path of natural development. Because she did not believe in forced learning by children, Montessori referred to her approach to education as an "aid to life." Its focus is always the development of the human personality, not the acquisition of information.

If education is to begin at birth, parents must be considered the child's first teachers. Montessori believed that parents needed and wanted help in this regard. A major goal of Montessori schools is to be a place where parents can go to get the information necessary for understanding children in each stage of their development. Ideally, Montessori schools begin with parent-infant classes. These weekly classes help the parents to prepare the environment of their home for their newborn children and each succeeding level of their development. Parents learn how to collaborate with their children in enabling them to use this prepared environment for their own formation. They are guided in giving the freedom to their children that leads to a developing responsibility.

When some of these classes involve visits to each other's

homes, parents learn from each other. They see for themselves that it is possible to solve the problem of giving their children freedom of movement by eliminating cribs and playpens without endangering their children's safety or their own peace of mind. They realize that it is possible to eliminate the clutter of unnecessary objects that we have begun to accept as part of our modern society but which are so damaging to the children's development of concentration and organized thought. They begin to buy toys based on their simplicity, beauty, durability, and possibility of repetitive and creative use. They see ways in which they can organize their homes to help their children's drive for independence: a child-size glass in a bottom kitchen cabinet, a small pitcher of milk on the lowest refrigerator shelf, low hooks on the bathroom door for hanging towels and pajamas, and so forth.

When children are able to walk with stability Montessori believed that they were ready for extensive exploration outside the home. The Young Children's Community is a prepared environment for children up to three years old in the Montessori school. For many parents it is a good place for this future exploration to occur. It has the advantage of being prepared solely for children under three years old, and it involves a community of children guided by adults who are focused entirely on the children's needs.

Ideally, in the Young Children's Community approximately ten children are together each morning for three uninterrupted hours. There is one trained Montessori teacher and an assistant. The materials of this prepared environment are based on activities of the home: cooking, cleaning, washing, flower arranging, and so forth. There are puzzles and manipulative games and objects to aid the children in the development of their senses, hand control, balance and coordination. Stories, songs, books, and picture cards of flowers, animals, and items of the environment, often for matching with miniature objects, encourage the development of language. Most of all, being together in this specially prepared environment helps children to develop an awareness of their own rights and limits, as well as the rights and limits of others.

Parents are sometimes hesitant to have their child spend five mornings a week outside their home. Montessori certainly did not think it was a requirement for children under three years to attend a Montessori school. On the other hand, children who do attend the Young Children's Community receive many benefits. The following remarks are those of a mother of an eighteen-month-old girl just a few weeks after entering a Young Children's Community.

> It seemed as if her vocabulary doubled overnight. There must be some kind of a spurt in brain growth going on. It's so extreme, it can't be anything else [referring to her experience in the Young Children's Community.] She has a heightened awareness and interest in everything around her. She goes right to Mrs. Anthony with her arms out. She is as happy to be with her as with me or Helen [her occasional sitter]. She knows Helen and she loves her but she would never go to her like that. It must be because of the situation. Mrs. Anthony offers her something no one else can [the Young Children's Community and its special environment].

When a child enters the Young Children's Community, parent education sessions continue but on a less frequent basis than the parent-infant classes. The goals of these sessions remain the bonding of parents with each other for support and the realization that the school is there to help them assist their children's development at home.

Parents learn that two of their most important functions for children under three years are to help them to independence and to set limits for them. Rushing in to help before children have asked for assistance ties child to parent. Montessori stated often, "Every useless help to a child is an obstacle to development." Parents are encouraged to set limits fairly and consistently, based on cultural expectations of behavior and the children's health and safety. They learn that when children sense no hesitation in their parents, they soon give up badgering them. Two-year-olds accept the constraint of a seat belt, sitting at the table to eat, or going to bed, because the determined, if gentle, manner of their parents gives them no hope of manipulation.

Very importantly, parents are encouraged to observe their children. In doing so, they begin to recognize Sensitive Periods and human tendencies of behavior at work in their children's lives. They develop ways to encourage, rather than ignore or actively fight, these aids of nature. For example, twenty-month-old children are in the Sensitive Period for order. They may respond vehemently when disrupted in developing orientation toward the use of objects and their place in the environment. Knowing this, parents can respond with less exasperation when children persist in returning objects to their accustomed place.

I know a child of less than two years old who insisted on wearing her winter coat outside, even into the warmer months. She consistently put the tissues that her mother had folded and put on a little table next to her potty for use as toilet paper back in the box. She became upset when her mother had no bike helmet one day because she had given it to her six-year-old brother, who had forgotten his for their bike ride together. These are all normal acts for a two-year-old in the Sensitive Period for order.

The importance of parents giving full attention to their children when possible, not for the purpose of entertaining them but to establish a collaboration with the children in their development, is also stressed. The energy of the child under three years is such that parents usually find time together a challenge.

The following incident illustrates this point. A mother of a twenty-one-month-old boy said to me recently, "It's just incredible how much time he takes. It's so hard to get anything done but take care of him. I want to be there for him but it is so frustrating when there are so many things that I want to accomplish." Then she told me that earlier that day she had been in the yard with her son. He had begun to climb up a five-foot open-rung ladder that was leaning against a tree. After he got to the top, it was extremely hard for him to get down. At first, he tried to turn around and face outward, so that he could see where he was going. He kept trying to figure out how to turn his body around, how to look forward while going down backward. He worked at this for a long time. Finally, he gave up trying to turn around and began to descend backward, clutching, with his chubby hands, the ladder rung, dropping one foot down then feeling for the rung below. Eventually, when he found it, he started feeling for the next rung. He was totally absorbed in his activity, concentrating every muscle. Sometimes he missed a rung and hung there, feeling about with his foot. His mother remained next to him, holding her arms out to "spot" for him.

Each time that he missed, she resisted the temptation to place his foot on the rung. It was hard not to help, but he was so pleased with himself when he managed on his own and gave no indication of wanting help. All the while that he was engaged in this concentrated effort, he was repeating to himself, "Don't fall, don't fall," "Be careful, be careful," "Climb down, climb down." When he made it to the bottom after such laborious effort, he said, "Do it again!" and up he went. This process continued for an hour and a half. Then he stopped as suddenly as he had begun. Some inner need was met. He was calm and happy and ready to go inside for his lunch.

Knowing that behavioral tendencies were at work in her son during his activity of exploring, orienting, making an order of movement, manipulating his hands, repeating for perfection and precision, communicating his actions, helped this mother to take the time to collaborate with him in his climbing efforts. They involved far more than developing his capacity for climbing a ladder. They had to do with his self-formation of skills, not for a gym class but for life.

After describing this incident to me, the mother said, "I was so glad that I could take this time for my son that morning." Of course, it is not always possible for parents to give such help in their children's development. It is important that they do so when they can, however. The rewards are as great to the parent as to the child, both now and in the future when the child grows into a strong and independent adult.

As the children in the Young Children's Community approach three years old, they begin to show signs of readiness for the Children's House, the primary classroom for children ages three to six years. At home, they are somewhat calmer in appearance and behavior. After the earlier period of such intense discovery and exploration, they seem almost to be resting, as if to catch their breath. They are less demanding and easier for the adult to cope with. Montessori believed that they were passing from the unconscious to the conscious Absorbent Mind and ready for sensorial experiences of a more refined type.

Montessori designed a prepared environment for these children that goes beyond the Young Children's Community and the replication of the home it represents. This new environment serves as a bridge to the outside world for the children. Montessori could not put the world in one room for the children to discover but she could place "keys" to its exploration there. These "keys" are given in four areas: practical-life materials, mirroring activities of the culture, such as care of self and the environment; manners, and social behavior; sensorial materials, reflecting the qualities and facts of the world; and mathematics and language materials. All of these materials are for individual use and encourage each child to continue sensorial exploration of the real world.

The primary classroom consists of twenty-five children ages three to six with one Montessori teacher and a nonteaching aide. By necessity children in such a large group learn how to get along with others, to respect their rights, and to share an environment where there is only one set of any particular material. There is no forced social learning or grouping, however. Children of this age continue to be ego-centered in order to serve their self-formation as individuals. This goal is respected and served by the environment.

When the children first enter the Children's House, they are busy with the practical-life materials. Through them, they further develop their concentration and their ability to be independent. They also continue to learn the manners of their culture through grace and courtesy lessons. These are not "lessons" in the usual sense. The teacher demonstrates how to walk in front of someone or set a tray down quietly or blow a nose. Because the children have Absorbent Minds, they spontaneously copy the teacher's modeling of behavior. The older children also serve as models for the younger ones in this regard.

It is not long after entering the primary classroom that the new children become interested in using the sensorial materials. This is particularly true if they have come from the Young Children's Community where they have had opportunities to develop their capacities for concentration, effort, and organization.

The sensorial materials are each designed to convey an abstract idea in concrete form. Sound cylinders for shaking and matching and, eventually grading their sounds, convey the concepts of loud, louder, loudest and soft, softer, softest. Musical bells to strike and match and, later, to grade and convey tone and pitch. Sandpaper tablets give the experiences of rough, rougher, roughest and smooth, smoother, smoothest. A tower of cubes demonstrates volume and size; a series of rods, the concept of length, and so forth.

When feasible the sensorial materials are composed of sets of ten objects, giving the children an indirect exposure to the basis of the decimal system. They also represent specific measurement designations and geometrical shapes. Ten rods represent variations in length, ranging from one decimeter to a meter. A hexagonal box shows that a hexagon can be made of equilateral triangles, trapezoids, and rhombi. The exactness of these materials appeals to the human tendency for precision and gives the children an experience of the realities upon which human technology is based. All the sensorial materials involve the use of the hand in a classifying act. The hand and the brain act in unison making a mental connection between an abstract idea and its concrete representation.

The teacher presents each sensorial material to the child the first time, giving him or her an experience of its purpose. The child is then free to use the material whenever he or she wishes, always returning it to the shelf carefully and in its former order. It is in this subsequent use of the material by the children that substantial learning takes place. The teacher encourages repetitive use of the materials in various ways while, at the same time, being mindful not to overcontrol or overdirect the children. The aim is to arouse a spontaneous response to the materials.

The final act in the use of the sensorial materials is the attachment of language to the abstract idea that a particular material represents. Language transforms the knowledge gained into a "key," which the children can use for further exploration in the world outside the classroom. They see the sky or a flower or bird and recognize that the color of each is blue. They discover that a particular bird is a darker blue than the sky and the flower a lighter blue. They not only recognize these comparisons but they can communicate their discoveries to others with the appropriate terms: light, lighter, lightest and dark, darker, darkest, and so forth.

Language is always taught to the children in the Séguin Lesson. This is a learning process of three stages developed by Dr. Edouard Séguin. It involves relating a fact or concept to an object—for example, "big"—then naming the fact or concept and asking the child to find that piece of material, as "Where is 'big'?" Finally, after a number of experiences, the third stage is tried, "What is this?" If the child can name the correct piece, "big," it is an indication that the idea of "big" is now within his or her mind and a tool for further exploration. The advantage of learning in this manner is the flexibility that it provides. The second stage, which is the actual learning period, can be extended and repeated as many times as necessary for an individual child. Each child then has a greater chance for success in the last period, which is, in effect, the testing stage.

The sensorial materials establish a solid basis for the language and mathematical materials to follow. The materials introducing literacy and numeracy (numerical understanding) to the children do not represent subject matter for the children to "learn" in the usual sense. There is an initial presentation of the materials in an ordered progression. This procedure appears similar to regular education in that the teacher imparts information. The difference lies in the recognition that this merely awakens the child to specific information. It is in the follow-up practice, spontaneously undertaken by the child, in which learning occurs. Montessori is very clear on this point. Learning is made possible for the children, it is not forced.

By being introduced to, and allowed to explore and discover, the language and mathematics materials that Montessori prescribed for the prepared environment, the children reach an unusual development by the time they are six years old in both literacy and numeracy. In language, the children can write their own stories in cursive and illustrate them with pictures and paintings. They read real books, rather than the customary primers for first and second graders. They have an understanding of the function and placement of words in sentences as a precursor to grammar and analyzing of sentence structure. They have studied word types, such as antonyms, homonyms, contractions, and compound words. In addition, they know many language facts: facts of geography, such as land and water forms and names of countries on each continent and their flags. They know facts of nature, such as the names of flowers, trees, animals, birds, and fish. They learn many facts of art and music history, such as names of paintings and artists and musical pieces and composers. They discover facts of social history, such as the clothing, tools and shelters of peoples of the past and of other parts of the world today. All of these facts become a basis for the children's further curiosity and independent research studies in the elementary level.

In mathematics, the children establish a solid basis for understanding the decimal system, the role of zero within it, and the hierarchy of numbers to the millions. They have a strong foundation in the four mathematical operations: addition, subtraction, multiplication, and division. They have begun the memorization of the math facts and tables. They have built a strong base for geometry through their sensorial exploration of quatrefoils, ovals, ellipses, polygons, and triangles (including the names of their sides and angles). They have experienced algebra in concrete form—both the binomial and trinomial theorems—and are ready to discover them in the abstract in the upper elementary level when they are nine to twelve years old. Through counting and labeling, squaring and cubing chains of small bead bars, the children become familiar with skip counting (3, 6, 9, 12, etc.) and establish a foundation for discovering square root and cube root, again to take place in the elementary years. They have worked with fractions and discovered that they can do all four mathematical operations with fractions as easily as with whole numbers.

These intellectual achievements of the children are impressive to adults. However, they do not represent what is most important about the Children's House and the children's self-formation there. It is the children's development of personality and social behavior which is the essential aspect of Montessori education. The children's good manners, their gentleness with each other, their confidence and ease with those both younger and older than themselves, including adults, their care with their environment, and their eagerness and energy for learning, make clear the potential of the Montessori primary classroom.

It is not just the thoughtful preparation of the physical environment and the materials and activities there which bring about these positive results in the children's behavior. It is the social composite of the classroom. Montessori always included children spanning three years of age in her primary and elementary environments. She stated that "Even if we had over a thousand children and a palace for a school, I would still think it advisable to keep together children with an age difference of three years." The combination of various stages of the children's development "makes possible the best individual formation."[5]

The indirect learning that occurs among children is a primary reason for placing of children of different ages in one environment. The youngest children are guaranteed models for more mature behavior than they themselves are capable of performing. The older children have opportunities to develop their potential for leadership and social responsibility. This indirect learning occurs in the intellectual area as well. Younger children observe the older children work with materials that they will use in the future. Older children spontaneously help the younger ones with materials that have already been introduced to the younger children but which they have not yet mastered.

Many people misunderstand Montessori's approach to the children's social development at the primary level. They think that her emphasis on the children's formation as individuals in the first plane of development is an indication that she considers social interaction between the children to be of secondary importance. This is not true. In fact, she insisted that young children must be in a community of others to develop to their full potential. She wrote:

> A question that is frequently asked is if children [under age six] develop individually in our methods, how can they be prepared for social life? This would lead one to suppose that society is composed of individuals who are not developed. . . . If the children develop individually, they do not live as hermits. . . . We must see the individual in his or her place in society because no individual can develop without the influence of society. . . . The human individual cannot develop without a social life.[6]

By including twenty-five or more children from ages three to six in one environment and giving them freedom to move about and talk with each other at will, Montessori created a positive "influence of society" for the children within the classroom.

Montessori used the environment in another way to further the children's social development. She purposefully placed one set of each group of materials in the classroom. She explained,

The material is a help because we have only one set of material in a class so if one child is using the piece that another child wants, the latter must wait until the first child has finished with it and put it back in its place. . . . The children do not give the material to each other but always put it back in its place when they have finished. So they have an exercise in patience and respect for others. All these little things help. They bring sympathy and understanding. It gradually brings a real harmony which could not be given artificially.[7]

In addition, the children's social relationship with adults is enhanced by the inclusion of children of three different ages in the classroom. The children then remain with one teacher for a total of three years before going on to the next level. The possibilities for depth of relationship, positive influence by the teacher, and modeling of behavior are greatly increased. Further, it is possible for the teacher to relax and enjoy teaching each child. There are three years in which the child can reach the goals for formation. The teacher can be patient and have faith in each child's natural rhythm of development.

It is significant that Montessori did not consider the unusually high level of social and intellectual formation which children reach in the Children's House beyond their normal capacities. In fact, she believed it was evidence of their normal development for individual formation and the encouragement of natural behavioral urges common to all human beings. When, after the initial weeks of adaptation to the Children's House, the children's responses began to reflect the social and intellectual behavior which I have described, Montessori referred to the children as "normalized."

"Normalization" invariably follows in the classroom when the children begin to "work" seriously with a material or activity. When Montessori first observed this phenomenon in San Lorenzo, she was surprised. No one, at the time, equated children as young as three years old with a desire for concentrated work. Yet, the children in San Lorenzo showed such an interest. Montessori observed that when this desire is satisfied, children become calmer and appear rested and content. They are more compassionate with each other and they exhibit increasing responsibility for their environment.

It is true that the children's affinity for intellectual work needs particular materials and a prepared environment to bring it to full fruition. However, if the children are given freedom with these special means as a point of contact, they consistently exhibit love of order, concentration, and exactitude. Montessori eventually witnessed these phenomena in children all over the world and from every type of background. She concluded that "It is by work that children organize their personalities."[8]

It is important to understand that Montessori made a clear distinction between the work of the child and the work of the adult. Failure to comprehend this key distinction makes it difficult to grasp the significance of Montessori's revolutionary discovery. Although work is important to both adults and children to maintain harmonious personalities, children's work differs in scope and purpose. Adults work to change the environment; children use the environment to change themselves.

This is not to deny that children love to play or that play serves an essential element in their development. There is a misunderstanding among preschool educators and Montessori advocates in this area. Dr. Mario Montessori, Jr., a psychoanalyst and grandson of Maria Montessori, addresses this controversy in his book, *Education for Human Development.*[9] He discusses the fact that play is a self-expressive activity. It appears to be essential for the full development of the child. However, there is no need for an adult to be active in this process. It is self-contained activity with the structure of the play determined by the child's perception of reality. On the other hand, there are essential activities that do require adult assistance. These are those experiences for the child's development that involve learning something new about the exterior world. These activities appear to satisfy the child to a different degree and to meet unique needs in personality formation beyond those of play alone.

Montessori believed that it was only by seeing the children in her classrooms that adults could understand the phenomenon of human development and how it is assisted by her educational approach. She wrote, "It is the children themselves who finally make people really believe in it [an education based on the planes of development, human tendencies, and activity based on interest]. They are the last and incontrovertible argument for it."[10] Seeing their children thrive socially and intellectually in primary classrooms has prompted parents to explore Montessori's ideas about the second plane of the child's self-formation and the benefits of continuing Montessori education for their children at the elementary level.

3

△ △ △

CHANGES AT THE
SECOND PLANE

The second plane of formation lasts from the child's sixth to twelfth year. Montessori education for children does not vary in basic approach or educational procedures during this period. Therefore, elementary classrooms at both levels, from age six to nine and from age nine to twelve, are essentially the same. Montessori observed startling changes in children beginning at approximately age six indicating both a new goal and a new direction in their development. The children's focus shifts from individual formation to development as social beings and the direction of their explorations of the world tends to the abstract rather than the concrete. All the children's behavioral tendencies serve these new purposes.

In addition, new powers appear in the children to facilitate these revolutionary changes. These powers are both physical and intellectual. The mental powers of the earlier period, the Absorbent Mind and Sensitive Periods, are replaced by new intellectual endowments. Montessori referred to these new attributes of the second plane as "psychological characteristics." Many of these psychological characteristics correspond to the earlier "Sensitive Periods" in that they direct the child's interest to specific aspects of self-formation. They do not, however, have the same selective time frame, nor are they so exclusive in focus and interest as the definitive periods of the first plane.

Physical changes in their children are often the first ones to be noticed by parents. The children's baby teeth fall out and permanent teeth grow in. Their legs grow longer and their bodies become thinner and taller. Their heads are smaller in comparison to their bodies, and their bodily proportions begin to resemble more closely those of the adult. Their physical health is more stable; many childhood diseases are over and the crises of the adolescent years are in the distant future. The children's new physical strength and stability gives them great stamina and energy. They are adventuresome and "rough and tough." They enjoy overcoming obstacles and have a new fortitude in facing challenges.

Mentally, the children have an immense power and are capable of great effort and concentration. Their intellectual curiosity is limitless. This curiosity is not the same as that of the adults. A scientist, for example, seeks to find something new. The children's purpose is the formation of their own minds. They take in new information in order to re-form it and bring it into existing relationship with what is already there. Recent research substantiates this conclusion of Montessori. The frontal cortex of the brain is not a storage place but is in constant formation and re-formation, in interaction not only with the outer environment, but within the brain's own interior pathways.

Montessori called this stage of the child's formation the Intellectual Period. The children's appetite for knowledge is immense. They are not satisfied with bits and pieces of isolated information: this part to write a report on, that part to memorize and reproduce for a test. They want to grasp the whole of knowledge. Montessori wrote that in this period "All other factors . . . sink into insignificance beside the importance of feeding the hungry intelligence and opening vast fields of knowledge to eager exploration."[1]

It is at this age that the children first begin to distance themselves from their families. Montessori described this separating as an "attitude of detachment from the home environment. . . . What the child likes best is to go out. The limitation of home and its protection become irksome."[2] It is not the family which the child seeks to leave behind but his or her role as a child within it. Children begin to move away from the security of their families and their role as children who accept their parents' expectations of them usually without protest. Parents notice that their children who were happy to visit adult relatives in the past no longer want to accompany them. Children stop caring very much about their appearance and are contented to be dirty rather than clean. Their good manners of earlier years become unpredictable. It is as if the children realize that they cannot remain with their families forever. It is time for them to strive for further independence in both action and thought.

In spite of this distancing of children from their families, it is quite clear that they feel no less love for them. Typically, they are affectionate and generous; they are often more comfortable, however, if the initiative comes from themselves. The children now tend to join together and form their own peer group outside of the family. They become more extroverted; they want to be with other children and to be like them.

They experience more than a gregarious urge. The children

want to be together in organized activity. They choose a leader and follow a purpose. Montessori describes this phenomenon as "a form of association for more developed persons. Little children [under six years old] go along harmoniously by themselves but juniors . . . need a different kind of organization . . . which would have been useless for the little children who were at a different stage of development."[3]

The children play social games and establish groups that expand their experiences with new rules. They seek evaluation by their adherence to these new standards of conduct. By adult perceptions these new rules can be very strange. They often involve secret languages, passwords, special dress, hidden treasures, hideouts, and bizarre rituals or mannerisms. At the same time, the children want privacy from adults. It is as if the children are exploring the group process itself and, in this way, are rehearsing for adult society.

As the child's Absorbent Mind disappears, a new way of relating to the environment and a new power of mind becomes manifest. It is the functioning of the environment and the relationships within it which arouse the children's interest. They pester us with constant questions of "how," "when," "where." These questions are not the child's "why" questions of the earlier plane. Younger children ask "why" but they are in effect asking "what," "what is that," "what is it called." In other words, they are searching for facts rather than the reasons behind those facts. This is clear in their response to the reasoned explanations that adults often try to give to children under six years old. When we begin involved answers to the younger children's queries, we suddenly find that the children are off and about, leaving us quite alone with our lengthy renditions.

There is nothing wrong with giving very young children reasons in answers to their questions. This may help them to develop sound reasoning abilities later, just as surrounding uncomprehending infants with language helps them to develop their own language at a later stage. However, this is not usually why adults give young children such reasons. Too often we expect young children to comprehend and, more often than not, to remember the reasons given or at least to reason through to the answer for themselves in a repetition of our reasoning process. Persistence of adults in this regard can lead to extensive problems in parent-child communication.

Now in this new period children have developed the higher brain function required for reasoning. Unfortunately, this is often just the time when parents, frustrated for several years with giving reasons instead of facts to the younger child, conclude that it is hopeless to give reasoned explanations to children. Our answer now to the older child's "why" becomes "because I said so."

What does the reasoning power specifically permit us to do? Reasoning allows us to keep facts and ideas in relation to each other. We can compare, deduce, and arrive at conclusions. The reasoning capacity shows itself clearly in the children's new interest in searching out the interrelatedness of things. They explore all the facts which they have absorbed sensorially in their earlier years. Now they begin to ask "why" and "how" in search of the relations between these facts.

Montessori describes children on the threshold of reason as

entering into a new world, the world of the abstract. It is
a rich world in which the acts accomplished by human

beings will interest them more than the things. . . .
Before they were interested in things. Now they will occupy themselves mainly with the how and the why. All
that used to attract them sensorially now interests them
from a different point of view. They are looking for what
needs to be done. That is, they are beginning to become
aware of the problems of cause and effect.[4]

With this power of reason, a new world of independent thought
and discovery is opened up to the child. It is the realm of abstract
ideas that now intrigues them. The child of six years of age has
become a reasoning explorer of the abstract.

The children's new interest in the abstract extends to the
development of a moral sense. Elementary-school children continually question what is right and wrong. Their ultimate goal is
not the facts of right and wrong as perceived by their parents.
They want to use their newly developing powers of reason to
come to their own conclusions about right and wrong. This is a
process of discovery that initially involves questioning their parents in some detail about their responses to particular situations.

A consequence of this search for information in the moral
realm is a phenomenon which adults often refer to as tattling.
Children of this age continually report the behavior of other
children to adults. The persistence and frequency with which the
children do this can be aggravating to adults. Reflection, however, reveals the relationship of this behavior to the children's developing moral sense and reasoning power. Their interest is in
distinguishing right from wrong. They are seeking clarification
from the adult: "Is this a bad thing to do? Should I accept this?
Why?"—or, conversely, "Is this a good thing to do? Should I try

to do this, too? Why?" Eventually, children decide on their own code of morality. When this occurs, they have no need for the adults' reassurance in this area. Consequently, they cease to badger the adult about the behavior of others.

The children's interest in judging behavior extends to a new interest in justice and compassion for others. Montessori wrote,

> It is at six years that one may note the beginning of an orientation toward moral questions toward the judgment of acts. This preoccupation belongs to an interior sensitivity, the conscience. . . . It is at this age . . . that the concept of justice is born, simultaneously with the understanding of the relationship between one's acts and the needs of others.[5]

The children not only want to discern just from unjust acts. They want to fight against injustice whenever they become aware of it. Montessori described the children as having a "keen feeling towards injustice. When the adult demands from young children something that they cannot give, it is always the six year old that comes to their defense. This rebellion towards injustice is general; it extends even to animals."[6]

A companion characteristic to the children's interest in morality and justice is their tendency to worship heroes. They have an intense interest and admiration for great men and women who have pushed to the limits of human capabilities. However, they relate more readily to their feelings than their intellect in this regard. It becomes important to help the children develop awareness of the realistic versus the unrealistic acts and needs of others.

One of the greatest new powers to appear in the second plane is the children's capacity for imagination. Because adults tend to confuse the young child's propensity to fantasize with the powers of imagination, it is important to clarify the differences. Montessori does not regard the credulity and fantasizing of children under six years old as evidence of their intellectual powers of imagination. Very young children readily believe that animals can speak in human voices or that inanimate objects can move and think, for example. When children reach the second plane they become keenly interested in whether these ideas of theirs are true or not. Earlier they could not distinguish whether what they were being told was so. Now they have their own reasoning powers. They ask themselves if what they believe is true and test their conclusion against discernible facts.

Montessori maintains that imagination is a development of higher consciousness and is dependent upon a prior ability to distinguish fact from fantasy. This capacity to discern reality first makes it possible to discover the interrelatedness of facts, thoughts, memories, wishes, and so forth. The formation of imagination is rooted in sensorial experience. It is the ability to picture material objects or real experiences in their absence, to see in the mind what we no longer see, to hear what we no longer hear. We take these images and make new mental creations from them. However, in order to do this we need to have had previous experience of these images.

Newton saw the apple fall and Einstein the trains approach and then fade in the distance, and each through these experiences used his imagination to discover new aspects of the universe and its manipulation through technology. Montessori wrote, "Imagination does not become great until human beings, given the courage and strength, use it to create. . . . Obstacles abound in the world but human beings' mental lives (including their powers of reason and imagination) give them the strength to surmount them."[7]

Because a rich sensorial experience is a necessary foundation of a fully developed imagination, Montessori believed that, in general, a concentration on reality versus fantasy is more useful to the very young child. However, it is incorrect to assume that Montessori saw no role for fantasy in the child's life. For older children she believed that fairy tales, myths, fables, and other uses of fantasy should play a key role in moral understanding and exploration of feelings and emotions. Her grandson relates that she told him such stories when he was younger than the age at which she suggested them for other children. It is probable that it was the adult's tendency to overemphasize fantasy in the young child's life that led Montessori to minimize it to such a degree in her lectures and writing.

Montessori spoke eloquently of the role of imagination in human history and proposed that it be the major avenue for introducing the children at the second plane to their further education. In 1948, she said,

> Human consciousness comes into the world as a flaming ball of imagination. Everything invented by human beings, physical or mental, is the fruit of someone's imagination. In the study of history and geography we are helpless without imagination, and when we propose to introduce the universe to the child, what but the imagination can be of use to us? I consider it a crime to present such subjects as may be noble and creative aids to

the imaginative faculty in such a manner as to deny its use, and on the other hand to require children to memorize that which they have not been able to visualize. . . . The secret of good teaching is to regard the children's intelligence as a fertile field in which seeds may be sown, to grow under the heat of flaming imagination. Our aim therefore is not merely to make the children understand, and still less to force them to memorize, but so to touch their imagination as to enthuse them to their inmost core. We do not want complacent pupils but eager ones; we seek to sow life in children rather than theories, to help them in their growth, mental and emotional as well as physical.[8]

The primary classroom allowed the children's human tendencies to follow their natural inclination to operate through a sensorial exploration of facts and to utilize the children's unique mental powers of absorption and sensitivity to precise aspects of the environment at specific time periods. Now changes in the children at the second plane make it clear that they are no longer interested in exploring the same things in the same way, nor do they any longer possess the same powers to do so. The new psychological characteristics appearing in the children enable them to concentrate for the next six years on their development as social beings. All their interests and energies, their human tendencies and urges to activity, now serve this new goal. Montessori's task was to design a new plan of education that could meet this challenge.

4

△ △ △

The Great Lessons
and Key Lessons

ontessori proposed presenting the whole universe to
the child in the elementary years. The universe holds
within it the answers to all questions. Such an all-
inclusive context can meet the challenge of the child's great intellectual curiosity and strength at this age. She wrote,

> Let us give them [the elementary children] a vision of
> the whole universe. The universe is an imposing reality
> . . . all things are part of the universe and are connected
> with each other to form one whole unity. This idea helps
> the mind of the child to become fixed, to stop wander-
> ing in an aimless quest for knowledge. The child is satis-
> fied, having found the universal center of self in all
> things.[1]

Montessori stated that for the elementary child, "the power
of imagination is what educates." It was the imagination that she
chose as the avenue for her elementary plan. She designed five

major stories and numerous minor ones to introduce the universe to children. The facts of these stories represent the truths of the universe as we know them, but they appeal to the child's imagination to comprehend those facts and their meaning.

Montessori designed her first story to present the whole of the universe as a framework for all the children's later knowledge. Each succeeding story carries the children into further and further detail, arousing their curiosity and interest along the way. These stories are not to give all information that could be given. They give just enough to create the beginning of an interest. This interest expands and grows as the child develops with each passing year. Montessori wrote,

> Looking around us at the cultural development of our epoch of evolution, we see no limits to what must be offered to the children, for theirs will be an immense field of chosen activity, and they should not be hampered by ignorance. But to give the whole of modern culture has become an impossibility and so a need arises for a special method, whereby all factors of culture may be introduced to six year olds; not in a syllabus to be imposed upon them, nor with exactitude of detail, but in the broadcasting of the maximum seeds of interest. These will be held lightly in the mind, but will be capable of later germination, as the will becomes more directive.[2]

Giving the children the universe as a context for their further study solves the problem of the children's accumulation of isolated bits and pieces of knowledge with no way of relating one to another. The children's power of reason is stimulated to search for the connections between all things. Gradually from one detail the children become interested in another. Montessori wrote, "Interest spreads to all, for all are linked and have their place in the universe on which the mind is centered. The stars, earth, stones, life of all kinds form a whole in relation with each other, and so close is this relation that we cannot understand a stone without some understanding of the great sun. No matter what we touch, an atom, or a cell, we cannot explain it without knowledge of the wide universe."[3]

There are educational reformers from time to time who hope to free children from the tyranny imposed by a curriculum chosen by others and force fed to them. They often suggest that children should be free to study whatever they like. This is not what Montessori proposed. She wrote "Some new educationists . . . advocate giving them [children] freedom to learn only what they like, but with no previous preparation of interest. . . . The necessity for the child . . . is help towards building up of mental faculties; interest being first of necessity enlisted, that there may be natural growth in freedom."[4]

The purpose of Montessori stories is to provide this necessary "previous preparation of interest." It is possible then for the children to follow their own path of discovery with a large measure of freedom. Montessori realized that in order to pursue their education in freedom, children would need more than a "preparation of interest" given through stories. They would need the *means* for further discovery through their hands and brains working in unison in independent activity. In the Children's House, this means for discovery was represented by materials on the classroom shelves: "keys to the world," Montessori called them.

Now in the elementary level, Montessori again devised materials for the children's explorations. These new materials represent "keys to the universe." As in the primary environment, these materials appeal to the children's human tendencies to explore, to find order and orientation, to manipulate and repeat precise movements, controlling the error, until relative perfection is reached. However, the elementary child's tendency is to explore the abstract. These elementary materials then build upon the abstractions already developing within the children through their earlier work with concrete materials in the Children's House. For example, the concept of the triangle is carried much further in the elementary level through an analysis of its parts. Again symbols are given to the pieces of the Binomial Cube which are familiar to the children because of repeated previous manipulation in the primary level. These symbols, "a" for the large cube piece, "b" for the small cube piece, enable the children to discover the algebraic formula which the Binomial Cube represents,[5] and so forth. The elementary materials then become in reality "symbols of symbols" for the children.

Montessori is unique in elementary education in the degree to which she gave materials to the hand for manipulation. Parents entering a Montessori elementary classroom see immediately upon the shelves the whole of their child's path to independent discovery. This visible representation of knowledge to be explored is a surprise to most parents who are accustomed to an elementary curriculum that is hidden away within prescribed textbooks and workbooks. Nor do the materials on the shelves in the elementary classroom represent the set curriculum of regular education, timed and measured to fit the calendar and required of all children, regardless of their individual interests and capacities. The materials are the means to personal formation for each child. Not every child will work with every material to the same extent, and some children will go much deeper in their search for knowledge in specific areas than others.

The materials on the shelves lead the children to exploration beyond the classroom walls, out into the community and world beyond: to libraries, museums, universities, parks, observatories, botanical gardens, zoos, concert halls, homes of local residents who are knowledgeable or gifted in a particular field of study, and more. The children's opportunities to learn are not bound by the materials in the classroom. They are as limitless as the children's desire to know. The children's Absorbent Minds and Sensitive Periods led them to a sensorial exploration of the materials at the primary level. Now, in the elementary, a new means has to be used to appeal to their desire to explore. That new means is the framework of stories which Montessori devised to appeal to the children's imaginations.

Although Montessori's plan to stir the children's interest while presenting material directly to them—as opposed to imposing a set curriculum—sounds radical to us, it was not an entirely new idea. As long ago as the seventeenth century, John Amis Comenius (1592–1670) wrote in *The Foundation of Modern Education*, "Education should appeal to the child's natural interest. Whatever is to be known must be taught by presenting the material directly to the child."

Montessori's five major stories dramatize the known truths of the universe and the progression of human civilization. They present in turn the creation of the earth, the beginning of life, the coming of human beings, and the tools of human communication, that is, language and mathematics. The law and order of the universe gradually become clear to the children through each successive story. The interrelationships within the universe, which these stories convey, are a major reason for their appeal to elementary children. Children's minds are not divided into categories. They operate as whole systems. Nor is the universe divided into subjects. The mind delving in one area of study automatically comes into another. Six-year-old children have advanced to the state of observing and being intrigued by this phenomenon. Montessori believed that it was important to use this development in the children's intelligence in their elementary education: "It is necessary to make use of the psychological state which permits the view of things in their entirety, and to let them [the children] note that everything in the universe is interrelated. Thus, when the children want to understand everything, the world which they have before them can fill the need."[6]

Montessori called the five major stories the Great Lessons. In reality this term is a misnomer. These are impressionistic stories, accompanied by simple experiments, teacher-made charts, time lines, and illustrations. The children are not to memorize the facts of these stories and then reproduce them for the teacher, as the term "lesson" would imply. The lessons' purpose is to create a picture in the children's minds and to send them off wondering, questioning, and exploring in order to fill in the details of that picture. Their response in the days following a story should always be "You said this. What about that? What comes next? Isn't there more?" If the teacher is successful, this inquisitive searching to fill in specific detail will continue throughout the children's lives.

The teacher is careful not to ask his or her questions of the children. Only when children seek to answer questions which they themselves ask, do they commit themselves to the hard work of finding answers that are meaningful to them. This emphasis on the children's questions versus our own is often difficult for adults. Nevertheless, the teacher is to give only as much guidance and encouragement as is necessary to elicit the children's interest. This concept is the basis of Montessori education and the means whereby it reaches its goal of leading the children to lifelong learning.

In the first Great Lesson the teacher tells the children that "in the beginning it was very, very dark, darker than they could ever imagine and that it was so cold, much colder than they had ever been. It seemed as if there was nothing there at all in this very dark, very cold space that was everywhere. But eventually, there was something. . . ." Montessori designed four impressionistic charts and six simple experiments to aid the children's imaginations as the teacher continues the story, describing how minerals and chemicals were the first "actors" in our universe; how they formed the elements, fire, water, and air; how matter transforms to three states of solid, liquid, and gas; how particles joined together and formed the earth; how heavier particles sank to the earth's core and volcanoes erupted sending molten rock, ashes, and vapor into the atmosphere; how mountains were formed and the atmosphere condensed into rain, creating oceans, lakes, and rivers.

Geography is thereby introduced to the children within a framework in which all details of life can be traced. In the following days, the children repeat the experiments accompanying the story on their own. They begin to ask more and more questions. "How cold is it in space?" "Why don't the planets fall on earth?" "Why are those closer to the earth going faster?" and so forth. Older children go deeper and deeper in their studies: the composition of the earth leads to a study of its layers, and the folds in the earth's crust to the isostatic balance and the study of plate tectonics, for example. All further studies and the children's future questions and discoveries spring out of this original story and introduction to creation.

Today this first Great Lesson is usually referred to as "The Creation of the Universe and Coming into Being of Earth." Originally, this story was called "God With No Hands," and many Montessori teachers still refer to it by this title. Therefore, it is important to note that neither the first Great Lesson, nor any of the subsequent stories, supports a specific religious approach; they favor neither the creationist nor evolutionary theories of the earth and the life upon it. They are in fact compatible with all major religions and theories of creation.

Montessori had respect and tolerance for all religious views. As an anthropologist and student of human societies she was familiar with the varying expressions of religious belief throughout human history. She spoke particularly of her respect for the Eastern religions and their recognition of the frailty of the balance of life's forces. Their meditative approach to life may well have influenced her recognition of the children's need for the "silence game"—a game, practiced in the Children's House, which involves the cessation of movement and mental concentration. Montessori met with Mahatma Gandhi both in India and Europe and corresponded with him. The encouragement of the children in Montessori elementary education to pursue their own interests and to make independent judgments we hope will lead the children to explore all the religions and philosophies of the world.

The second Great Lesson is called "The Coming of Life." It

tells the story of life on earth and introduces the children to the study of biology. It begins by presenting, in an impressionistic manner, the story of single-cells and then multi-celled forms of life. It explains how these forms of life became embedded in the bottom of the sea and formed fossils. A time line accompanies the story. It traces the Paleozoic, Mesozoic, and Cenozoic periods, beginning with the kingdom of trilobites and ending with human beings. The teacher indicates on the time line where vertebrates began, followed by fish and plants, then amphibians, reptiles, and birds and mammals. There are no dates on this time line. The goal is to give the children an idea of all that went on before human life appeared. This impression stirs their imagination and desire to know more.

After presenting the story, the teacher invites the children to examine the time line more closely and answers some of their questions. If the questions involve longer answers, the teacher says, "We will talk about that in a day or two" or she might even make a definite appointment with children to do so. She leaves the time line on the wall for a period so that the children can go back to it. It is not to be a permanent fixture there, but it is always available to the children somewhere in the room.

On the classroom shelves, there is a corresponding blank time line with pictures sorted and organized in the various sections of the original time line. The children can take out one section of the blank time line and an envelope with a group of pictures. The children build up their knowledge gradually until they can complete the entire blank time line. In addition to the other related biology materials on the shelves, the teacher selects a few pertinent books for research and puts them in strategic places in the room for the children's discovery.

After a day or so, the teacher can go back to the story picking up on a few details or adding more facts. One period can be discussed in further detail. Again the children may want to know more about the animals on the time line. The teacher can introduce names of groups or classifications, various groups of invertebrates, the group of cephalopods, gastropods, sea anemones, and jellyfish—the last two still alive today—or discuss what happened to the trilobites, which were once so numerous. The teacher can introduce facts about climate. The icicles on the time line represent the ice age. What effects did these periods of glaciation have on various life forms? The teacher can explain that a period of glaciation was generally preceded by a rising in the land and a reduction in the amount of surface water. This can lead to a study in other areas of geography—water, ice, glaciers. As before there are materials on the shelves to further the children's exploration and discoveries on these topics.

One idea ties together all of the presentations of this time line of life: As each of these life forms was living out its life, satisfying its own existence, it was contributing, at the same time, to the environment and making it possible for other life forms to exist.

The third Great Lesson introduces human beings and their unique endowments: intellect and will. There are no special time lines, charts, or illustrations to accompany this story. The aim is for the children to imagine what life was like for early humans. This lesson is called "The Coming of Human Beings," and it introduces the children to the study of history and the progress of human civilization.

Each of these first three Great Lessons is told in a manner that reveals the pattern and order of each new form of creation and the existence that was special to it. The endowments of human beings made it possible for them to be the creators themselves of the last two stories: the beginning of letters and numbers.

Preceding the presentation of the last two stories is an introduction of a time line called the "Hand Time Line." This time line presents the concept of prehistory to the children. It is a three-meter-long strip of black felt with a hand represented in the middle. While unrolling it for the children, the teacher explains that for a long long time human beings lived on earth—doing things with their hands, caring for their children, working together—before they wrote down anything about what they were doing. At the very end of the time line, the teacher comes to a strip of red felt one centimeter wide. This narrow strip presents the proportionate period of recorded human history. Montessori's emphasis on prehistory is unusual in elementary education. Perhaps it was Montessori's background in anthropology that caused her to recognize its importance in the context of our overall existence on earth.

Exposure to prehistory makes it possible for children to realize that numbers and letters were not always part of human life. Someone had to create them. Since letters and numbers are now common all over the world, every group of people must have invented written symbols to represent their ideas and their calculations. It is stressed for the children *why* it was important for human beings to do this. They discuss how a group of people moving about together might want to tell another group about the location of a poisonous snake or about buffalo to kill for their skins and meat.

Sometime after introducing the Hand Time Line and the

importance of communicating ideas and quantities with written symbols, the teacher gives the fourth Great Lesson. It is called "The Story of Communication in Signs." It begins with a discussion of the Egyptians, who had two kinds of symbols: one for ideas and one for sounds. These symbols were simple pictures. At first, they carved these pictures in stone, but later they used a brush and made a kind of paper from a plant that they found near the River Nile. The story goes on to describe the Phoenicians as a busy group of traders, who used the "sound pictures" of the Egyptians but not their "idea pictures." The children are intrigued to learn that the sandpaper letters that they learned in the Children's House came from these early signs carried by the Phoenicians. Next, the contribution of the Hebrews, Greeks, and finally the Romans, are introduced. The children discover that the pre-Greek origins of the alphabet are Semitic, from the Hebrew *aleph-bet*, but that the Greeks were the first to call the twenty-six letters of the Phoenicians the "alphabet." This part of the story has meaning for the children because of their work with the Movable Alphabet in the primary classroom.

"The Story of Communication in Signs" represents an introductory experience for the youngest children, who are just developing their understanding of reading and writing. The older children go into more depth, studying different alphabets and kinds of writing, such as Egyptian hieroglyphics and American Indian picture writing. Often they investigate the origins of paper and writing utensils, the printing press and its influence in history—and, today, the computer and fax machine.

The last Great Lesson is called "The Story of Numbers." Its introduction emphasizes how human beings needed a language for their inventions, so that they could convey measurement and how things were made. The story tells how some people counted only one and two or one, two, and three; but most counted more, possibly using their fingers to do so—just as young children do today. Some groups of people used stones and notches on sticks to record their numerations. A chart accompanies this story showing how the Mayan people used stones for counting and how they might have used a pile of stones to leave a message about how many animals they had seen in that place. The story continues with the Sumerians and Babylonians who had a number system based on sixty. The children learn that the Babylonian number system is the basis for our sixty-second minute and sixty-minute hour. Finally Greek, Roman, and Chinese numerals are introduced.

The story explains why our numbers are called Arabic. They are similar to numbers found in a cave in India from two thousand years ago. The Arabs, who were a great trading people, brought these Indian numbers to the rest of the world. These Indian numerals had something that no other number system had: the zero. Again, this story has meaning for the children because of their experiences in the Children's House with specific materials that introduced the concept of zero and the decimal system. Through this last Great Lesson the children develop a sense of the continuity and interdependence of human history and an appreciation for those unknown people who have made our present state of human civilization possible.

To make clearer how the Great Lessons appeal to the children's imaginations and set a stage for their future discoveries and studies, the third story is recounted here in synopsis form. It is presented to the children within the first four weeks of school. Since the Great Lessons are the framework for all the children's explorations and study, it is important that they be recounted early in the school year. All the stories are given within six to eight weeks of school's start.

△ △ △

For each Great Lesson, the teacher gathers together all of the children who are new to the class. Older children who have heard the story before are invited to join in. Many, if not most, will do so. Older children who hear the story for a second, third, or more time, gain something new at each telling. With each narration, the children have an opportunity to pursue an interest different from the previous hearing and to undertake different studies afterward in response to their own questions.

When presenting a Great Lesson, the teacher summarizes briefly the ones that have come before. Therefore, he might begin the third Great Lesson by recounting that, in the first story, the children had heard about how the earth came into being and, in the next story, how life started. The teacher might remind the children of the time line of life, which showed all the different creatures that have lived on earth. The teacher then begins the new story telling the children that "it is very special because it is our story. It is called 'The Coming of Human Beings.' Just as today, these human beings were men, women, and children. These human beings had special powers that made them different from all the other animals, just as we do today. They were able to think. We can think, too, like those first human beings."

The teacher encourages the children to think about their own minds and about all the things that they can think of in their daily lives. They discuss the first human beings on earth and what they could feel and see and think about. He might say, "When the wind blew and it made them cool, early humans could think about that, and when the rain came, they could wonder what made it happen and where it came from. At night, they could see the pattern of the stars. These first men and women could make up stories about all these things as they thought about them. They could tell these stories to their children for them to think about, too."

The story tells about another of the special capacities of human beings: "the ability to love in a different way than all the other creatures who care about their young." The children discuss how they can love their mothers and fathers, brothers and sisters, families and friends. The teacher might continue, "This very different ability to love involves caring about people that we cannot see and may never know. We want all people on earth never to be hungry or sick or in need."

Not only do the capacities of thinking and loving in a special way make human beings different, but we are also able to do a great many things that plants and animals cannot do because we are freed from a preordained way of life. The teacher explains that animals and plants can only do certain things. The children then discuss some examples: the cow eats grass, the squirrel eats nuts and acorns, birds eat insects, worms, and berries. The teacher continues by encouraging the children to think of the many different things which they eat, how varied are their shelters, clothing, and so forth. He reminds the children of the picture cards that they worked with in the Children's House and which depicted the variety of foods, clothing, and shelter of human beings today and in earlier times.

After introducing the abilities of thinking and loving, the

teacher begins a discussion about one more special human endowment: the human hand with its thumb and forefingers that can form the pincer grip. He might say, "There is still another very special capacity which we are given. We have hands that can do things. Even early human beings had hands and were able to walk on two legs, so that their hands were free to make things. So let's just think for a minute about some of the things that we can do with our hands." After some discussion, the teacher might end by saying, "Imagine if you had to crawl around all day on your hands and knees and do these things!"

This Great Lesson arouses the children's curiosity about human beings and what they have been doing since they first appeared on earth. The teacher tells them that there are many more stories about human beings which he can tell them, just as he has been doing lately about the earth, plants, and animals.

Because the purpose of the Great Lessons is to arouse the children's imaginations, they are not followed with assignments in reading and writing designed to measure what the children have "learned." No books are handed out with ready-made stories and pictures. Nor are the children pressured to get something with which to occupy themselves. Instead the Great Lessons are always followed by what Montessori called "the rest." The children are left alone for a period of calm and reflection to think about what they have heard and seen. In the days following a Great Lesson the children's questions about what they have been told become the avenue for their further studies.

The manner in which the children carry out their continuing explorations in the Montessori elementary environment is as revolutionary as the idea of introducing the whole universe to six-year-olds through their imaginations. In regular schooling, children in the first grade are often seated at separate desks, given their own textbooks or workbooks, and instructed to do their own work. They may not even talk with each other. Most damaging of all to their relationships with each other, they are not allowed to help each other and are forced into competition for grades, prizes, class ranking and often are measured on a "curve" system. The children in Montessori elementary education have a very different experience. They are free to work in groups, talk with each other, and help each other.

In the Children's House, the children work as individuals developing their personal capacities. The goal in this independent activity is logical. According to Montessori, "It is very evident that the need to help others or to seek their collaboration cannot manifest itself when one is convinced of one's own inadequacy . . . vital energies consist in the sense of one's true value and in the possibility of participating in a social organization."[7]

Now that the children's foundations as individuals are strong, Montessori encourages the elementary children's new inclination to explore—to ask questions and search for answers, to find order and discover exactness, to fashion materials with their hands, to repeat until relative perfection is reached, and to communicate the results of their work as part of a team. In this manner, the Montessori elementary plan uniquely meets the children's need in the second plane to form themselves as social beings, capable of contributing to others, both following and leading in group effort.

In the primary classroom, there is a low buzz of sound accompanying the children's individual activities as they work and talk quietly, side by side. In the elementary environment, there is an expanded bustle of activity and sound. The excitement of synergy is in the air as groups of children work together at large tables or mats on the floor, do science experiments, compose music on the Tone Bars, carve wood, or paint an illustration for a story or time line.

In the days after a Great Lesson, the teacher's goal is to get groups of children researching for the answers to their questions and doing their work together. The Great Lessons alone cannot accomplish this aim, however. A Great Lesson only opens the door to a general area of study: geography or history, for example. Given in isolation these stories do not give the children sufficient information to follow specific interests in these general areas.

For this purpose, Montessori devised additional stories to follow the initial telling of the Great Lessons. She called these stories which presented further detail in a particular field, the Key Lessons. Key Lessons make possible the explorations which were indicated in the Great Lessons but, without the additional information which Key Lessons provide, the children could not carry out. The Great Lessons present the whole; the Key Lessons expand on their details with key information.

There is a crucial balance in the amount of detail to be given in the Key Lessons. If the children of this age are bombarded with detail, they do not seek out information on their own. In the second plane, the children's maximum strength and energy urges them to stretch themselves. It is this "stretching" of their capabilities that rouses their interest and results in activity. There are many interesting facts and variations that could be offered to the children but, if they are not absolutely essential to understanding, they can become obstacles to initiative and independent thinking. The teacher learns to sense this needed balance for each individual child and group of children.

The Key Lessons are not all given to every child or in any

particular time frame. Each child comes with his or her own interests and capacities. The Key Lessons are the means to help each one reach his or her personal potential. The teacher chooses Key Lessons to give to groups of children based on observation of their interests.

Because there are many small groups of children within the classroom following different lines of activity at any one time, the children are simultaneously exposed to a variety of studies. Ideally, each area of study represented by the Great Lessons is being actively pursued by some of the children at all times. The constant stimulation by the numerous activities and ideas of others around them accounts for the unusual breadth, as well as depth, of knowledge that the children ultimately achieve.

The follow-up studies which the Key Lessons make possible for the children always involve written or spoken language experiences. Sometimes these experiences result in charts, time lines, dramatic presentations, or written and oral reports. Often these are shared directly with other classmates or given in a formal presentation to the class as a whole. Sometimes they are shared with the younger children in the primary classroom or other elementary classrooms. This sharing of information with others helps the children's knowledge to become fixed in their minds through a natural and effective means.

The number of Key Lessons which extend from the Great Lessons varies. For example, the third Great Lesson, "The Coming of Life," has five Key Lessons. These stories are accompanied by two charts called "The Fundamental Needs Charts" and three time lines representing the three stages of human civilization: nomadic, agricultural, and urban. A description of one of these stories gives an indication of how such a presentation can give the children enough information to begin a new exploration and inspire them to do so without dictating a particular field of inquiry.

Because this is a period for social interest and exploration, elementary children are fascinated by the uniquely different ways in which human beings throughout history have fulfilled their fundamental needs for food, clothing, and shelter and secondary ones for transportation and defense. There is another area of discovery for the children as well. From the beginning, human beings were not satisfied merely to have shelter for survival. They sought to make their shelters beautiful. They were not content with bowls alone but attempted to make them of a pleasing shape and design. They also made music and created dances. In addition, burial rites and religious beliefs were part of human life from its inception. There are special customs, behaviors, morality, and religions which belong to every culture. There is, then, a spiritual territory of common humanity for the children to explore, as well as a physical territory.

The Key Lesson called "The Fundamental Needs of Human Beings" tells the children a little about these needs of human beings and their ways of fulfilling them. Enough is told to rouse the children's imaginations, but no more. At the end of the story, the children are shown a fully illustrated chart on one of the physical needs of human beings: the food chart. This chart gives the children an idea of how they might go about recording and researching just one of the needs of human beings that the Key Lesson has introduced. There are no other premade charts.

The children are now free to explore, selecting one need that is of interest to two, three, or four of them. They gather information from books in the classroom, the local library, or any other source which they decide to investigate together. They work together to make a report, chart, or some other depiction of their choosing. At the end of their research, they have a beginning concept of the varieties of human behavior in meeting fundamental needs over historical time periods and in geographic locations. Their discoveries lead them to further questions involving more detail: How did climate affect the food eaten or the tools used or the availability of animals? The children discover that all human beings, from the beginning of time, have had and will have the same needs. Their view of the world is changed. When they look at a picture of a man and woman in a *National Geographic Magazine* or people in books from another part of the world, they realize that they share bonds of common needs and interests. Their differences lie in the different ways in which they meet these needs and interests.

Research in the physical and the spiritual aspects of needs lead the children in a natural way to explore the universe itself— all life within it and the interrelationship of human beings with plants and animals. The final result of presenting the universe in the open-ended manner of the Great Lessons and the Key Lessons is freedom for both children and teachers. The children are no longer bound by the adult's concept of what it is useful to know, a concept that, in any case, has no power to arouse their interest. The teachers are freed from the "teach, learn, test" formula that represents much of regular education. Their task is made easy, for they no longer have to decide upon a syllabus and then drag the children through it. They are free to follow and build upon the children's own interest.

Speaking at the University of Amsterdam in 1950, Dr. Montessori said,

It should be realized that genuine interest cannot be forced. Therefore all methods of education based on centers of interest which have been chosen by adults are wrong. Moreover, these centers of interest are superfluous, for the child is interested in everything. A global vision of cosmic events fascinates children and their interest will soon remain fixed on one particular part as a starting point for more intensive studies. As all parts are related, they will all be scrutinized sooner or later. Thus, the way leads from the whole, via the parts, back to the whole. The children will develop a kind of philosophy which teaches them the unity of the universe. This is the very thing to organize their intelligence and to give them a better insight into their own place and task in the world, at the same time presenting a chance for the development of their creative energy.[8]

The educational goal of Montessori elementary education is to develop within the children a global vision. Montessori calls the path whereby this goal is achieved "cosmic education." The Great Lessons and the Key Lessons and the connection between the two are the means whereby the teacher activates cosmic education in the elementary classroom.

The result of cosmic education for the children is a developing gratitude for the universe and their lives within it. They form an awareness that they have received many gifts from human beings whom they will never see or know. Children take for granted that what they see around them has always been there. They need help in understanding that once there was a time when even the simple enhancements of their lives—pencils or forks, for example—did not exist.

The fact that most of the things that we take for granted to-day were once the creation of some person whose name we do not even know is significant to the children. There is wonder in their voices as they speak of the contributions of others that they have discovered in their research. This wonder and appreciation for persons unknown but so important in their daily lives helps the children to realize that they, too, can make a contribution to the world. Appreciation for the universe itself is based on the knowledge that it was not always there. Through the Great Lessons and Key Lessons, the children become aware that the universe evolved over billions of years, and that it is based on the law and order through which all the plants, animals, and the rest of creation are maintained. Gradually they understand that they are part of this order and participants in the ongoing life of the universe.

5

△ △ △

THE CLASSROOM
ENVIRONMENT

Montessori made the following statement in England in 1948: "We claim that the average boy or girl of twelve years who has been educated until then at one of our schools knows at least as much as the finished high school product of several years' seniority, and the achievement has been made at no cost of pain or distortion to body or mind. Rather are our pupils equipped in their whole being for the adventure of life, accustomed to the free exercise of will and judgment, illuminated by imagination and enthusiasm. Only such pupils can exercise rightly the duties of citizens in a civilized commonwealth."[1]

The success of Montessori education in meeting this claim in any specific situation depends upon its wise application in three major facets: the prepared environment; the prepared adult; and freedom with responsibility.

In the usual form of elementary education, the teacher teaches everything. In Montessori education at every level, it is always through interaction with the environment that the child learns; the teacher is only part of the environment. To meet such a challenge, it follows that the elementary environment cannot be haphazardly designed by an individual teacher's whim. Its structure must be "scientifically planned and methodically formed."

There are two elementary classroom environments: one for children ages six to nine and one for children ages nine through twelve. The arrangement of these classrooms is familiar to anyone who has experienced the Montessori primary environments. There are special materials displayed on shelves in an organized manner by sections: mathematics, geography, science, art, music, language, and so forth. The number of items is purposefully limited. Each one is carefully thought out for its aim and use. The materials are colorful but the baskets, trays, and containers which hold them are natural so as not to detract from the materials themselves. Glass jars and bottles are used to reinforce the logic and simplicity of utilizing objects that can be recycled.

Just as in the primary classroom, there are no multiple sets of materials. It is important for the children to feel that the materials of their environment are unique and special and well worth waiting one's turn to use. Similarly, in their explorations of living things—plants and animals—there is one of each category: one bird, one mammal, one reptile, and so forth.

The use of computers in the children's research and subsequent projects is a new component in Montessori education. To date it appears that children six to nine years old develop best when their hands are more directly involved with manipulating materials in their work. It is essential during this period that the children learn to think clearly and read and write in an organized manner. Computers are therefore not included in the prepared environment for use in research studies and creative writing until the upper elementary level where the children are nine to twelve years old. By this time, the children's thinking, reading, and writing abilities have a solid foundation. They are ready to make full use of the practical advantages of computers. The principle of limitation, however, still holds. Even if funds and space are available, there should be only a few computers in the prepared environment. These computers can function for each type of use: one which is part of Internet or other connecting system for doing research; one for writing; and perhaps another for developing multidimensional images (CAD/CAM) such as might contribute to architectural or design work. This minimal number of computers assures that the children become familiar with the capabilities of computers without missing the intellectual and social development that the other materials of the environment are meant to facilitate.[2]

The elementary classroom can best be described as a workplace. Although the noise level may be somewhat higher than in the primary classroom, the orderliness of the environment leads to concentration and careful effort. As in the Children's House, the overall effect of the prepared environment for older children is one of simplicity and harmony, thus inviting the children to its use.

The materials in the elementary classroom reflect the same creative design and simple beauty as those of the primary environment. Again, these materials are not the subject of instruction as visual aids or learning tools in customary education. Rather, the teacher familiarizes the children with the purpose and usage of these materials; learning takes place in their subsequent use by the children.

In the primary classroom repetitive use occurred with one material; for example, a three-year-old would use the Pink Tower—a set of ten cubes varying in volume from a decimeter to a centimeter—many times. A three-year-old will spontaneously build, dismantle, and rebuild this tower from the largest cube to the smallest cube over a period of weeks or months. Children repeat this activity on occasion when they reach four or five years old, in the manner of someone revisiting something known rather than discovering something unknown. In the elementary classroom, repetition is assured by representing the same principle—cubing, for example—with a number of different materials. Repetition is now assured by variety rather than by the sensorial appeal of one item, as in the Children's House.

Through their use of the materials, the children reach high levels of abstract knowledge and creative thought. Montessori believed that customary schooling did not carry the children nearly as far as they could go in their conceptual knowledge. For example, she said that the basic sciences can be well understood if they are presented to children in a manner that appeals to their imagination by using clear visual symbols. Introduced in this way, chemistry can interest children of nine years or even younger. Molecules, atoms, and formulas do not attract the children, but the forces which they represent or explain do. Children are interested to learn that in water "oxygens and hydrogens wish to remain united and they seek each other out. . . . Hydrogen has only one possibility of uniting, oxygen has two." This concept leads to the understanding that hydrogen has a value of one, called a valence, that hydrogen is univalent, oxygen bivalent, and so forth. Symbolic representations then show how compounds are formed, and in this way the children discover the relevant formula H_2O.

Montessori believed that "We can even bring the child some notions of organic chemistry. This is thought today to be more difficult, so that it is not taught before the student's entry into the university. This is a mistake. If some formulas of organic chemistry are presented in visual form, why should they be more difficult than others?"[3]

Montessori's attitude toward chemistry for the older children is reminiscent of her ideas concerning fractions and their use in mathematical operations by the primary children. The way in which the concepts are presented is the pertinent factor. Children understand fractions and their use readily in the Children's House because fractions are approached through a sensorial exploration and followed by their symbolic representation. Children at the elementary level understand chemistry because it is introduced in a manner that uses their imaginative powers and ability to visualize concrete symbols.

Part of the appeal to the children's powers of imagination and reasoning lies in the context within which the materials are introduced and then used. In the Children's House, the facts themselves as represented in the materials stirred the children's interest and started them working. This base for motivation is later transformed. The children's interest is aroused by the context within which facts are explored and by their relationship one to another. Montessori states it this way: "One thing has been well established in our experience, that facts are of less interest to the [elementary] child than the way those facts are discovered."[4]

Reflection makes it obvious that to understand the discoveries behind known facts, subject areas must be used in a connected manner. Therefore, the children are encouraged to use all of the materials in any interrelated way. If the children are researching the historical development of writing, they might get out science laboratory materials to analyze the papyrus plant and the inks which the Egyptians used. Or they might gather art materials to illustrate their findings in a book or a time line.

Often introducing materials in their historical context reveals their interrelationship. There are stories about the Babylonians, Sumerians, and Phoenicians in almost every subject area, for example. Placing the material in historical context appeals to the children's imaginations and helps them to see relationships in knowledge, for example, in the presentation of the Pythagorean theorem. Because of the nature of the material to be manipulated and explored, this material is presented to only a few children at a time, possibly two or three at most. The teacher begins by telling the children, "Pythagoras was a Greek who was born in Samos about 580 B.C. When he was nearly fifty years old he went to live in Italy near the city of Naples." The teacher might continue, "He founded a religious order, which meant that he spent much of his time walking about with other men like him in long robes and thinking about the divine order in the universe. Pythagoras and his friends were looking for harmony, which they found all about them. Pythagoras had studied music, especially the harp. He noted a relationship between the harmony in music and the study of mathematics. Other people of that time thought they could find answers to their questions about the universe in matter itself, but Pythagoras looked for these answers in numbers. Let's see what he found out."

The teacher then shows the children a metal plate demonstrating the Pythagorean theorem in two renditions of triangles and squares—one on the right side of the plate and one on the left side. The left side contains a white right-angled isosceles triangle with metal squares of different color next to the two sides and the hypotenuse. The right side shows a right-angled isosceles triangle but this time the squares are separated into triangles instead of being represented by a solid square.

The teacher takes the white triangle and reviews its parts by asking the children their names: hypotenuse, vertex, sides, or legs. The children then verify that the squares of the two legs of the triangle are equivalent by moving the pieces about. The teacher asks, "I wonder if these two pieces would fit into the square of the hypotenuse?"

The children cannot verify this with the single-piece squares on the left of the plate, but they soon see that they can do so by moving the square pieces separated into triangles on the right side of the plate. They verify that both of those models are the same size, then transpose them to prove the Pythagorean theorem—the square of the hypotenuse equals the sum of the squares of the two sides, which works equally well when they use triangles, rhombi, trapezoids, and hexagons. The children usually do this a number of times, talking to each other about what they are discovering. During this process, the teacher elicits from the children a description of their discoveries. The children realize and express the theorem in their own words.

Another day, the teacher shows the children a second metal plate which uses a right-angled scalene triangle in its center instead of a right-angled isosceles triangle. The children explore with it and discover that the same equivalencies hold with this different triangle. Sometime later still, days or weeks, the teacher might say to the children, "If you were going to label what you did, I wonder what the formula would look like?" The children on their own can discover $a^2 + b^2 = c^2$. The children continue working with the Pythagorean theorem, later using the same Triangular and Hexagonal Boxes that they used in the primary classroom.

In the upper elementary level, the children explore geome-

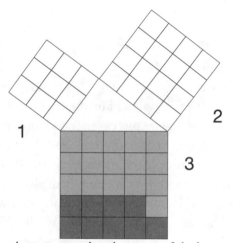

The Pythagorean theorem states that the square of the hypoteneuse equals the sum of the squares of the two sides. The darker squares in 3 = the 9 squares in 1; the lighter squares in 3 = the 16 squares in 2.

try by working with a sensorial depiction of Euclid's theorems. The ease and enthusiasm with which the children make these discoveries comes as a surprise to adults who were exposed to the same knowledge in a much different manner—usually in the form of an abstract theorem to memorize—and at much older ages.

Although the elementary materials are helpful to all children, they give maximum benefit to children who have attended the primary classroom. The Pythagorean Theorem Material is again a good example. Preparation for its use begins with the youngest children's development of control of movement, independence, will, and language through the practical-life and sensorial materials. After this initial development, the children are introduced to the Geometric Cabinet. This cabinet consists of a set of trays with wooden insets of squares, circles, triangles, and other geometric shapes to be explored sensorially, to be matched to cards and, eventually, graded by size. Next, they learn the language for these shapes: triangle, right-angled isosceles triangle, obtuse scalene triangle, acute-angled equilateral triangle, and so forth. Other materials, previously mentioned, can now be used: the constructive triangle and hexagonal boxes. Through these the children discover that equilateral triangles make rhombi, trapezoids, and hexagons, isosceles obtuse-angled triangles make parallelograms, an obtuse-angled scalene triangle and a right-angled scalene triangle can only make a trapezoid, and so forth. There is a final material called the "Superimposed Geometric Figures," in which children experience adjacent and concentric placement of graded triangle pieces and can make other geometric discoveries.

When the children arrive at the elementary classroom, they are well prepared, not only with a knowledge of triangles based on three years of exploration, but an excitement about the possibilities in future discoveries. The elementary teacher now gives many further presentations of triangles and geometric shapes involving the concepts of congruency, similarity, and equivalency. In their follow-up work with these geometric materials over several years, the children gain a progressively deeper impression of these concepts. It is to these "prepared children" that the teacher can present the Pythagorean theorem material and later the Euclidean material and be confident that the children can readily rediscover their meaning on a higher level of abstract reasoning.

The way in which all previous knowledge comes together at the end of each plane of development and makes further discoveries possible is a unique feature of Montessori education. This phenomenon is easily witnessed in the explosion of writing and reading at age six that culminates the work with letters of the three-, four-, and five-year-olds. Toward the end of the elementary level it is readily observable in the higher order of thinking that eleven- and twelve-year-old children possess. The teacher now can begin to ask the children to discuss what they think about a particular aspect of a Great Lesson or Key Lesson or a scientific experiment that they have just completed. She may ask them if they have ever seen a certain phenomenon as described in a Great Lesson or to write in a journal everything that they notice in their lives which has to do with something presented in a Great Lesson. After a week, the children can discuss what they have seen.

The children are now at a stage where their powers of reasoning make it possible for them to explore endlessly wherever their interests lead them. Because the prepared environment is designed to meet their interests at the highest level of abstract thinking, it is inexhaustible for children from ages nine to twelve, in the upper elementary level.

6

△ △ △

THE ELEMENTARY TEACHER

It is hard for adults to imagine that thirty or thirty-five children, from the ages of six to nine or nine to twelve, could all be working amicably and productively together in their respective elementary prepared environments without obvious outward control by their teachers. There are several factors helping to achieve this phenomenon.

The children coming from the primary class are well adjusted in their self-control. They now apply this self-control to working together in groups. This is not an automatic outcome. The elementary teacher lays the foundation for this result, just as the primary teacher had established the accepted patterns of behavior in the primary class.

There are significant differences in the approaches of the two teachers, however. Unlike younger children, who readily copy the teacher's actions, older children do not accept unthinkingly their teacher's modeling of expected behavior. Their reasoning minds question and challenge. The elementary teacher uses the children's new powers of thinking and imagining to involve them in a different approach to "grace and courtesy" lessons. The teacher uses drama and humor, creating scenarios. Because the children are now interested in a wider social environment, they role-play situations outside as well as inside the classroom.

The teacher might pretend to be in a library, banging down a book loudly on a table or carrying on a disruptive conversation. In an imaginary classroom, he might pretend to dominate a group project, telling everyone else what to do and refusing to acknowledge the ideas of others. The elementary teacher uses occurrences he has noticed within and without the classroom as a basis for illustrating behavior. Discussions of the children's behavior are extended into the moral realm. The psychological characteristics of children between six and twelve years old, discussed in Chapter 3, make it clear that this is a period for concentration in this area. Montessori believed that lectures on morality are of little use to children and can even have a negative effect. In regard to social behavior, children need to reason through to their own moral values. She wrote:

> A second side of education at this age concerns the children's exploration of the moral field and a discrimination between good and evil. They no longer are receptive, absorbing impressions with ease but want to understand for themselves, and are not content with accepting mere facts. As moral activity develops, they want to use their own judgment which often will be quite different from that of their teachers. There is nothing more difficult than to teach [by direct methods] moral values to children of this age; they give an immediate retort to everything that we say. An inner change has taken place

but nature is quite logical in arousing now in the children not only a hunger for knowledge and understanding, but a claim to mental independence, a desire to distinguish good from evil by their own powers and to resent limitations by arbitrary authority. In the field of morality, the child now stands in need of his (her) own inner light.[1]

It is through the realization of the human endowments, intellect and will, that children develop moral integrity. Their reasoning powers allow them to form their own judgments of good and evil; their will enables them to exercise the self-control to live by those judgments.[2]

Montessori's elementary education plan guides children to an acceptance of others different from themselves without trying to change these others to suit their own image. To accomplish the latter, the teachers are not to mold the children after themselves; rather, they are to guide the children to freedom and independence. She stated that, "If during the first period of development, the teachers have used very gentle methods and have intervened as little as possible in the activity [which was motor and sensorial] it is to the moral level that their gentle methods ought now to be oriented."[3]

The Montessori moral and spiritual approach to children is the same as in other areas of development—the teacher appeals to intellectual powers and psychological characteristics of the child's plane of development. At the second plane, this means that the teacher appeals to the child's reasoning mind and interest in exploration of society and those who have contributed to it, and the values of compassion and gratitude.

It is important to introduce the children to the heroes of their culture and the world, both past and present. They need positive examples of others who have contributed to society. Teachers can accomplish this awareness of heroes through books, stories, magazine and newspaper articles, films, visits to historic homes or sites, or visiting members of the local community. Exposing children to the exemplary lives and deeds of others inspires them to plan for the day when they can take their own part in the world as adults and give to others in their turn.

Social life within the classroom provides another natural opportunity for the children to discover moral values. Constantly working in a team and adhering to accepted classroom rules encourages exploration of moral attitudes. The informality of the classroom makes it possible for the children to discuss their relationships and behavior openly with each other on a daily basis. Facilitating the openness of such discussions is a primary responsibility of the elementary teacher.

There is a final element in the children's behavior that is the teacher's responsibility and is fundamental to the children's development in their attitude toward others, themselves, and the environment. Montessori's great discovery in the Children's House was that work is the road to normality for children. Work is not an option; it is a necessity for the development of what Montessori called the children's "normal behavior." This behavior is reflected in the children's cooperation and respect for each other and in their concentration and interest in learning about the world around them.

This same principle now relates to the older children; they have to work so that normalization of behavior continues. The elementary teacher's role is to serve as a link to the prepared envi-

ronment and the "keys" within it that arouse the children's interest in further work and discovery. The "seeds of interest" are to
give only an impression or idea that awakens the child's interest
in a specific area of study or subject matter. Once this interest is
aroused, Montessori believed, the children would be able "to
study and understand these subjects rapidly."[4]

If the teacher misuses the presentations and materials by
dictating to the children—telling them what areas to explore,
how they are to explore them, what they are to discover and
when—the children's behavior deteriorates. They lose their enthusiasm and energy and, one by one, they become increasingly
reactive and dependent upon adult monitoring and control.

To avoid this misuse of materials and to serve instead as an
effective link to the environment for the children, the elementary
teacher (as did the primary teacher) constantly observes the children in order to know where they are in their development at
any given moment. Both primary and elementary teachers keep
records of the children's activities, but the elementary teacher
goes much further in this process because the older children's advanced interests and development result in many more presentations to record. In addition, the children's follow-up work is now
very extensive and varied.

Elementary children are at an age when society has specific
expectations in educational standards. The teacher must keep
track of each child's progress as it relates to the local public-
school curriculum. In addition, standard tests, such as the
Stanford Achievement Test or the Iowa Tests of Basic Skills, are
administered yearly. Teachers use these tests as teaching, as well
as assessment tools, by going over them with the children question by question. This enables both teacher and children to iden-

tify individual strengths and weaknesses and to plan their work together accordingly. At the end of the children's six years in the elementary classroom, the teacher makes certain that the children have the academic skills and a general level of knowledge matching or surpassing those of their peers in the regular school system. Because the Montessori materials cover the standard school curriculum generally and, indeed, go much further in many instances, and because the children reach a high level of maturity in personal development, the children are well prepared, after completing elementary school, to enter the grade appropriate to their age of a public or other junior or senior high school.

Montessori left the format of student records up to individual teachers; however, she recommended that records be kept as simple and straightforward as possible. Elaborate records become increasingly time consuming and difficult to maintain. The only required standard is that they indicate exactly where the children are in their work, that the notations are up-to-date, and that they are accurate and clear.

Based on his daily record keeping, the teacher seeks to get two, three, or more children working together to explore an area of interest following a story or presentation of material. If a group of children appear to have come to a dead end in their search for information or process of discovery, the teacher steps in with just enough information to get them going again. He is constantly saying to himself, "These children were working on that last week. They got this far. How can I take them a further step in that direction?" Because the children are in a period when they have immense energy and curiosity, the secret to maintaining their interest is to keep them challenged.

As a general rule, the children choose their own companions for their work. The teacher's knowledge of social life is of little value to them. They need to discover for themselves, in this practice period of their lives when the consequences of their mistakes have no lasting effect, how to make wise choices in coworkers. Allowed to choose freely, the children gradually develop the ability to choose wisely. In particular, they discover that it is not necessary to work with their closest friends. Children of differing ages, sexes, and backgrounds work compatibly together, finding that diversity in companions leads to more varied and stimulating experiences than sameness.

When adult guidance is needed because a child is being ignored or treated unfairly, or children are not varying their coworkers sufficiently, the teacher provides a model experience for the children. She gathers together a preselected group of children, gives them a story or presentation, and sends them off to work together. Because the children are in an adventurous period in their lives, such a directed experience is usually sufficient to encourage them to enlarge their choice of companions.

When the children are concentrating and working independently and without teacher interference, they have achieved the goal of self-direction. The teacher leaves them alone and protects them from interruption. Montessori wrote, "We are concerned here with bringing them [the children] liberty and independence while interesting them in an activity through which they will subsequently discover reality. And for them this is the means by which they may free themselves from the adult."[5]

Montessori discovered that once children become self-directed, they do their best work when allowed a three-hour uninterrupted work cycle. Therefore, the elementary class period lasts for three hours in the morning and three more in the afternoon without ceasing for recess, gym, foreign language, art, music, or other events. Montessori schools that do not maintain this unbroken work cycle compromise the results of the children's education. There are many temptations to interrupt the daily schedule. Many adults do not understand its importance because the regular schooling with which they are familiar takes an opposite view of interrupting children in their work. In regular schooling, activities are changed constantly in hopes of holding the children's interest and reducing their mental stress. In addition, the time periods devoted to instruction have gradually been shortened over time. The unfortunate result is that expectations in academic achievement have had to be lowered correspondingly.

Montessori took a different view of the problem of motivation and children's mental fatigue. She said,

> The best they [the educators] could do was to compromise by reducing hours in instruction to the minimum, cutting out from the curriculum grammar, geometry and algebra, making outside play obligatory and postponing the age for entry into school. But however much free periods have been increased and children urged to play rather than study, strangely the children have remained mentally fatigued notwithstanding all these reforms. Montessori schools have proved that children need a cycle of work for which they have been mentally prepared; such intelligent work with interest is not fatiguing and they should not be arbitrarily cut off from it by a call to play. Interest is not immediately born, and if

> when it has been created, the work is withdrawn, it is like depriving a whetted appetite of the food that will satisfy it."[6]

Adults understand the concept of uninterrupted time periods with regard to their own activity. We can miss its importance for children's endeavors. Sometimes parents pressure Montessori schools to hire additional teachers to introduce various special activities into the classroom. These activities are often beneficial to children in and of themselves. However, their benefits are negated by their constant interruption of the children's work. The protection of the children's right not to be interrupted when productively occupied is key to the children's development of concentration and interest in their work.

To prepare teachers for the challenging role which she outlined for them, Montessori devised a thorough training course. Today, it is usually given as a nine-month graduate course after the teacher candidate has completed a bachelor of arts or sciences degree from a qualified college or university. Because the successive planes of development are the basis of Montessori education, it is important to have an understanding of the primary level and the child's development from birth to age six before studying the elementary level. Teacher candidates who do not hold a Montessori primary diploma are required to take a preliminary course summarizing Montessori theory for the primary child before beginning the elementary course.

The elementary training requires a solid foundation in the sciences, liberal arts and humanities, and covers all major subject areas. The aim is not for the teacher to become an expert in every field of study; rather, the goal is to become a "Renaissance person," sufficiently knowledgeable to arouse the children's interest in each area and to direct them to available sources for the answers to their questions.

The Great Lessons, Key Lessons, and materials to be presented to the children are covered in detail during the nine months of the course. An additional bonus for the teacher candidates is that many subjects encountered earlier in their education are often now understood on a deeper level. This is the result of experiencing many concepts on a concrete level for the first time. This is particularly true of mathematical ideas and formulas, which are customarily introduced to students in regular schooling through abstract representations.

In addition to working directly with the key materials, teachers-in-training, in effect, write their own textbooks, referred to in Montessori training as "albums." These albums are based on lectures and followed by practice with the Montessori materials. By creating their own "textbooks," teacher candidates develop a deeper understanding of the key materials. They also make the time lines, charts, nomenclature booklets, and many other handmade materials for use in their future classrooms. This hands-on experience leads to a more complete understanding for the teacher candidate.

Final written and oral examinations are given by specified International Teacher Trainers. Each trainee's album is inspected by a committee of both national and international trainers. The rigorous intellectual challenge of the elementary training course attracts young men and women who are sincerely dedicated to the education of elementary children.

In addition to the intellectual demands of the Montessori elementary course, teacher candidates are challenged in the area of personal development. The teachers are to be models for each of their children over a three-year period. Such a responsibility requires that teachers work to develop their character and interest in continued learning. Annual workshops, periodic required "refresher courses," and international congresses help teachers to deepen their understanding of education. Constant daily observation of the children not only deepens the teacher's understanding of the child's development but helps the teachers to develop the habit of self-observation and personal reflection. To become a Montessori teacher requires intelligence, enthusiasm, dedication, sensitivity, and faith in the children's development—qualities of good teachers everywhere.

Volume Material: Pouring sand from shape to shape introduces the concept of volume and the formulas used to find the volumes of certain three-dimensional shapes.

Racks and Tubes: This material demonstrates the roles of the divisor and the dividend in long division. Each tube contains ten beads that are color-coded to categories: units, tens, and hundreds.

Checkerboard: Children master the basics of multiplication working with bead chains on color-coded squares.

Pythagorean Material: Children see how the Pythagorean theorem works as they assemble squares along a triangle's hypotenuse.

Binomial Cube: Assembling the binomial cube allows children to experience algebraic formulas in concrete form.

Area Material: Children discover formulas for finding the areas of plane figures.

Flat Bead Frame:
Introducing a higher level of abstraction enables the multiplication of numbers to the millions.

Pin Maps: Children learn the names of countries as they place their flags on a pin map and check themselves with a printed map.

Grammar Box: The colored shapes of the grammar box are for mapping the elements of a sentence.

Time Line: On the time line of life, children discover when different forms of life appeared on earth from before the first Ice Age to the present day.

Charts: Charts of temperature zones and the spread of vegetation across the world raise questions about the ways that people adapt to their environment.

Daily Journal: The teacher periodically reviews the child's daily journal of completed work and work-in-progress.

Research Projects: Teachers assist in child-initiated research projects.

Story Materials: These materials inspire the children to seek out more information about mammals, reptiles, amphibians, birds, and fish.

Upper Elementary Classroom: Here older children are free to follow any interest with their own research, using resources from within and outside the classroom.

7
△ △ △

FREEDOM AND
RESPONSIBILITY

The final component leading to successful implementation of Cosmic Education for the children is freedom along with the capacity for accepting responsibility. The freedoms can be stated in a Bill of Rights for the elementary classroom:

> to act by oneself and for oneself
>
> to act without unnecessary help or interruption
>
> to work and to concentrate
>
> to act within limits that are determined by the environment and the group
>
> to construct one's own potential by one's own efforts

The elementary teacher takes special care not to violate these freedoms and assists the children in meeting the responsibilities which they engender.

The children entering the elementary classroom from the

primary level are experienced in choosing their own work and accustomed to the teacher's help in connecting to the environment through presentations of materials. Now both the children's independence in selecting work and their collaboration with the teacher in relating to the environment are extended. The children are given the means to keep track of their own activities and to be accountable for them.

When new children enter the classroom, the teacher gives each one a journal in which to record daily activities. Whenever possible these are bound journals from a stationery store. If available funds prohibit such a purchase, the children make a special cover for an ordinary notebook. Whether a bound book or covered notebook is used, it is essential that the journal be regarded as a special tool in the child's development. It must be attractive, carefully kept, and valued.

The teacher shows the children how to write the date and make time entries of their daily activities in their journals. It is important to note that the journal is a record of things that have already happened. It is not a plan for future work. As the children get older, they are encouraged to make comments about their work, and their journals become more extensive accounts of their ongoing development. When parents want to know what work their children have been doing, they not only can see the children's finished work; they can also read the written record of their daily activities. The father mentioned in the Preface whose son attended a Montessori elementary school emphasized the importance to him, as a parent, of reading his son's journals. He described in particular his reaction to his older son's journal, which gave him a glimpse into the child's mind and thoughts that he would have known in no other way.

In order to guide the children in the choice and manner of

their activities and provide an opportunity for individual attention, the teacher meets with each child periodically. Prearranged, one-on-one meetings with the teacher vary in frequency according to each child's needs. The most common arrangement is a weekly meeting. A few children may need meetings daily or every few days for a period of time; others may only need them bimonthly or even less.

These meetings give the teacher the security of knowing the progress of all the children. An equally important purpose is for the children to realize that the teacher knows how they are doing. The younger elementary children need the sense of security that this knowledge gives them. The goal of these meetings is for the children gradually to accept full responsibility for their own work.

Individual meetings are held during class time and are deliberately kept short. For the youngest children, they seldom last more than five minutes. For the older children whose work is more detailed and comprehensive, meetings may last as long as fifteen to twenty minutes, and customarily take place bimonthly or monthly. In their last years, there may even be some children who only need to meet with the teacher once a term. The frequency of meetings and the freedom given to the children in their work is dependent upon the development of each child's habits of concentration, effort, and discipline.

When the children come to their meetings, they bring their daily journals, completed work, and work in progress. A corollary to the meetings is that the children's file drawer or folder box, or other place they store their classroom work is cleaned out and straightened. At each meeting, the teacher goes over the child's journal, noting which group presentations were attended, what follow-up work was undertaken, and which materials or areas presented by the Great Lessons are not yet explored. The teacher is always certain to congratulate the children on carefully completed work and to draw their attention to what still needs to be done.

Besides assuming further responsibility in their work through their journals and individual meetings, the children extend their care of the environment. In the Children's House, the older children straightened, dusted, and swept their room for five- and six-year-olds. Now in the elementary level, the children take on nearly complete responsibility for their room. Wet mopping of the floors and additional cleaning of the bathrooms are the only major daily tasks not undertaken by children.

To reach this almost total responsibility for their environment the teacher leads the children through a series of steps. Elementary children have moved beyond the primary child's Sensitive Period for external order. They no longer carefully line up their papers or pencils in a row because of an inner desire, as they once did. It is reason that arouses the elementary children's interest in maintaining order and cleanliness. The teacher engages the children in thinking through the straightening and cleaning process in three phases. In the first phase, the teacher and children together draw up a list of all the areas that need care. In the elementary class, this list will include animals, plants, materials, furniture, and sometimes an outside environment of walks, gardens, or landscape.

The children choose the area for which each child will be responsible. The school day ends leaving ample time for straightening the room. First the children straighten their own work; then they help their companions do the same; last they clean the area of the room for which they are designated on a list. During this time the teacher makes certain that no child is taking a "rest" while friends do all the work.

After the children decide that all is complete, a team takes groups of children around the room on a tour of inspection. Phase one lasts until the children are able to straighten the room competently as a matter of course. When they recognize without being told by the teacher that the time for straightening up has come, it is a good indication that this first stage is complete.

In phase two, the children draw up their own list without adult help. If they leave any items out, the teacher does not mention it. Instead, all the children walk around the room checking the work. In this way, they become aware on their own of what they have left out. Each child again has a specific area of responsibility, preferably a different one from the time before. The teacher again waits until this second procedure becomes routine for the children.

In phase three, the children have the full responsibility of caring for the room on their own. At the end of the day, the children conduct tours of inspection to see how they have met their goal of a clean and orderly classroom.

When individual children have shown that they are responsible in maintaining the classroom environment, choosing their work with care, and working in harmony with others, they are each given a new freedom. This freedom comes as a surprise to adults, and it is difficult for us to comprehend its full import for the children. It involves freedom beyond their classroom environment and is referred to as "going out." As in the care of the classroom, "going out" is introduced to the children in phases.

At first, "going out" extends only to other parts of the

school building. Because many concepts considered in the elementary classroom are introduced with sensorial materials first encountered in the primary classroom, it is helpful for the children to revisit the latter and reacquaint themselves with specific materials. Hence, children from the six-to-nine-year-old class may come to the Children's House to borrow the red rods for a game involving concepts of measurement in decimeters and meters or children from the nine-to-twelve-year-olds' room may borrow the Binomial Cube for their discovery of the algebraic formulas which it represents. Sometimes the children search other parts of the building for examples of geometric shapes, or to measure rooms or to interview adults and children for a writing project.

When the children demonstrate that they can handle "going out" within the school building, they are permitted to go outside the building to the school grounds. They may be studying leaves or rocks or insects and choose to go outside to look for specimens. They might decide to include the school building in a study of architecture or a map of the school grounds or to follow some other interest that requires leaving the building.

After the children show that they can handle this added freedom capably, they are allowed to "go out" into the community beyond the school, first within walking distance and, eventually, to any commutable distance. Montessori wrote "To go out of the classroom in order to enter the outside world which includes everything is obviously to open an immense door to instruction."

To encourage "going out" activities, Montessori deliberately limited the resources within the classroom. For example, there are only a few select books with which to stir the children's interest in a particular subject. The goal is for the children to use the local library or other resources in the community to find the answers to their questions and complete their research projects.

In this way, the children become a part of the community at large. This is a natural process of social expansion which began with their moving beyond their homes and families to the larger context of the school. They now explore society beyond the school. Montessori described elementary children as having a need "to establish social relationships in a larger society. The closed school, as it is conceived today, can no longer be sufficient for them. Something is lacking for the full development of their personalities. . . . The closed environment [as in regular education today] is felt as a constraint, and that is why they no longer wish to go to school."[1]

Increasingly in the past thirty years, elementary children have been isolated from their community for the duration of the school day. Yet, it is in the second plane of development when children show their greatest interest in exploring their society. If elementary children experience the cooperative effort required for a functioning community, they develop a better understanding of the ultimate interdependence of all human beings as exemplified both in national life and international communications, commerce, and trade. This recognition of human interdependence has been a laudatory goal for previous historical periods. In today's technologically advanced world, it is an essential one.

The exploration of the community outside the classroom necessarily leads the children to an authentic discovery of the specific contributions that others are making to their society. The children come to see the necessity of the farmer for food, the storekeeper for exchange, the banker for commerce, the businessman for production, the policeman and fireman for protection, the workers at the sewage, water, and power plants for the operation of homes, buildings, and factories, the operators of road maintenance and public transit systems for transportation, and so forth.

A corollary to this understanding is the children's realization that human communities throughout the ages have been built upon work. The children develop an awareness of the meaning and value of work as the key to the continuation of all societies. They experience for themselves that every part of society has a role to perform. Each type of work is essential to the functioning of the whole. By seeing firsthand the workers of every kind in their community, the children come to the understanding that there is nothing demeaning in any necessary form of work.

The "going out" experiences further the development of the children's independence and will. Without a continuous development of these capacities, children are easily led astray. They lack confidence and do what others tell them to do, instead of keeping their own counsel. Just as the younger children in the primary class, the elementary children need to have lives of their own and not be overly dependent upon the adult.

The preparation that the children need to lead independent lives includes an awareness of life's dangers, as well as its opportunities. Three-year-old children in the primary classroom are shown how to use glasses and dishes that break, sharp needles and scissors that pierce and cut, hot irons and ovens that burn. Now, the elementary children need to identify and deal with the dangers which they may encounter in the larger society. They need to know how to respond to strangers, to deal with traffic, to take public transportation, to follow maps and street directions, what to do when help is needed, the importance of avoiding drugs and alcohol, and so forth. The teacher helps the children prepare for these situations through practice scenarios, stories, and discussions in which they reason through to their own solutions.

"Going out" experiences are always the natural outcome of the children's questions about their work and the need to research sources outside the classroom for their answers. They involve real work, not invented work camouflaging a desire for recreation or socializing with peers. Two to four children plan an outing together to continue their research on a specific topic or to purchase supplies for one of the classroom animals or to visit a local resident for a specific purpose. These are not field trips which involve the whole class and are organized by adults in order for the children to have a particular experience which the adults have chosen. "Going out" activities are always arranged by the children.

In order for the children to be as independent as possible in their organization of an outing, the teacher does a good deal of prior preparation both within the classroom and within the community. This preparation is similar in theory to the significant planning which the primary teacher must do in order to ensure the safety of the younger children in using potentially dangerous items, such as scissors and glass.

At the beginning of the school year, the elementary teachers alert the adults in the community of the children's possible presence during school hours. The teachers visit the local stores, library, and public buildings, including the park and police departments. They discuss with those in charge the behavior expected of the children on an outing. Their cooperation is enlisted in informing the school of any incidents needing adult attention.

Next the teachers familiarize themselves with the resources of the community that might be useful to the children. They prepare a classroom file of their findings and make it available to the children for reference. This file is divided by topics. In geography, for example, where the children might be exploring terrain, seasonal changes, and climatic effects, the teacher might list a planetarium, a local explorer, a telescope site, and land areas showing effects of sun, wind, or water. For biology, the list might include zoos, parks, botanical gardens, flower shops, garden exhibits, seasonal possibilities, such as ponds with tadpoles and dragonflies, gardens of sprouting bulbs, fields of crops, and vegetable gardens. The history file might include museums, archeological and fossil sites, homes of historic figures, historic buildings, statues, and commemorative tablets. For language, the teacher might list museums, libraries, homes of literary persons, poetry readings, films and plays. In mathematics, the list might consist of the mathematics department at a local college, an expert in the history of mathematics, and any exhibits or lectures by mathematicians. The music file might list concerts, operas, and homes of local musicians. In art, the teacher might include museums, homes of painters, local art studios, photography studios, special exhibits, art galleries, a pottery studio, and a weaver's home. The teacher keeps this permanent "going out" file current by periodically updating it. A separate file records temporary exhibits, films, and other events that might be useful to the children.

For outings that require an adult companion, an up-to-date

file is also kept of adult volunteers. These are parents, grandparents, friends, and neighbors of the school who enjoy helping the children. The role of the adult companion is to accompany the children in those situations where adult presence is deemed necessary. When the school is located in a safe community, adult companions are usually not necessary for local trips of short duration. For longer trips, an adult accompanies the children.

Outings to museums and other places of interest can be enjoyable experiences for adults. Recently, a parent described taking four children from our school to the Chicago Museum of Science and Industry. The children were working on a research project about the human body and wanted more information on the circulatory system. At the museum, they walked through the heart exhibit and then sat on the floor with their clipboards to write their impressions. The accompanying parent was standing to the side as the children worked. A visitor to the museum watched the children working for awhile, then he began talking to them. He wanted to know why they were not "having fun," racing about the exhibits, laughing, and talking like other school children who were there. "Museums should be fun!" he insisted. Finally, one of the children who did not look very happy about these interruptions stopped writing a moment and glanced up from the floor. "But we *are* having fun," he said in a polite but firm voice. He then went back to his work with his companions, concentrating as before.

The visitor, still looking puzzled, addressed the parent standing nearby. "Are you the teacher?" he asked. She explained her role, "The children have to research questions that they want answered. They have a specific idea in mind and they plan a trip to wherever they need to go. The art museum, or whatever it is, becomes an extension of their classroom." "What do you mean 'an extension of their classroom'?" the visitor asked. "The art museum becomes their library, their laboratory. It makes learning come alive for them. Knowledge is not just something in a book," she answered. "How often do they do this?" he asked. "It depends on what they have decided to do research on. This is the second time this week for this particular group," she said. "What a wonderful way to learn," he said as he looked back at the involved children, boys and girls together, by now lying on the floor, writing on their clipboards and obviously relaxed and contented.

If "going out" experiences are to have this positive outcome for the children, they need detailed preparation for specific outings. They need to know how to get where they are going, what to take with them and what behavior will be expected of them. When the children decide on an outing, the teacher goes over the necessary details with them—finding the address, using a map to locate it, going over the route including street crossings and traffic considerations, transportation, if it is not a walking trip, and so forth.

Because the goal in all of this preparation is both physical and mental independence, the teacher helps the children to make all the preparations for a particular expedition by appealing to their reasoning powers. She asks them questions, "How will you get there? What materials do you need to take? How much money do you need? What clothes are you going to wear? Do you need good walking shoes? What if it rains? What about meals? What are you going to find out? How does that fit in the work that you are now doing?" and more.

There is always a discussion of behavior expected in the situation to be encountered: how to behave in a music auditorium if it is a concert, for example. Montessori noted that too often adults assume that children know how to behave in society. They neglect to give them special preparation for specific situations. The outcome is frequently embarrassment for the children because they are ignorant of social expectations. As a result, they develop social insecurities and resentments. Sometimes their reaction is extreme and they revert to open rebellion against a society that has not helped them to become part of it.

The teacher's help to the children includes a discussion of what to do if they encounter adults who are rude to them. They stress the fact that if things do not go as planned, or if for any reason they feel uncomfortable, it is all right to come home without completing their plans.

When their planning with the teacher is complete, the children make the necessary phone calls. The trip is added to the calendar of upcoming events. On the day of the outing, the children always take a "going out" packet with them: a wallet with any necessary money, telephone numbers, a letter of introduction by the teacher, a letter of permission from the school administrator, an identification card with the school's name, address, and phone number, and medical and insurance information. After the outing, the children write thank you letters to those who made the trip possible or contributed to its success.

Unfortunately, compromises in the "going out" program, as Montessori conceived it, have to be made in schools in inner cities or other communities that are considered unsafe for children, even when accompanied by an adult. The benefits of Montessori elementary education are such that the children develop in independence, will, and social understanding, even without its "going out" component. On the other hand, the children are deprived of opportunities in social development that are rightfully theirs. This is why Montessori schools make every effort to overcome the obstacles presented in the children's exploration of their community through a "going out" program.

A final program in the elementary plan exemplifies the balance of freedom with responsibility that is the foundation of Montessori education from the children's earliest age. This program is called the Community Service Program and it is a culmination of the children's development as individuals in the Children's House and members of society in the elementary level.

Montessori believed that the children's final years in the upper elementary level were the natural time for the children to realize that they do not have to wait until they are adults to help others. This is a period when children have great compassion and sympathy for others. Being aware that they can give to others in need, aids the children's confidence and belief in their developing capacities.

The teachers prepare for the Community Service Program by researching the community for situations in which the children can be of service: to the elderly, younger children, the handicapped, or others in need. The children then choose whom they would like to help. The teacher monitors carefully whether the service the children are to offer matches their ages, interests, and abilities.

A father relayed the following incident which followed his son's experience in a Community Service Program. One winter evening after he and his twelve-year-old son had checked their bags at the curbside checking area at the airport, they saw an elderly man in a wheelchair sitting by himself. They could see that his family was having trouble managing all their bags and several small children. His son walked right over and said, "I would like to help you." He took the wheelchair and pushed it into the terminal alongside the other family members. The father said that he thought to himself, "Now why didn't I do that?" He was impressed with his son's confidence and ease of manner in talking to the older, infirm man but it was his gentleness with him for which he was totally unprepared. He remembered then that his son had spoken often over the last two years about his experience helping in the local nursing home as part of the Community Service Program at his Montessori school. He had not realized how deeply these experiences were influencing his son's development as a person.

The purpose of the Montessori elementary plan goes beyond the customary educational aim of developing the child's intelligence. Montessori believed that this is too narrow a goal for elementary schooling. There are many intelligent people in the world. Yet human beings remain far from solving the problems of survival on earth, either for ourselves or for our environment. Montessori believed that, in addition to intellectual achievement, education must help children to develop a sense of themselves and their place in the world. The second plane of development is the prime period in which to begin such an education. The children are in a relatively stable stage, physically and emotionally. The reasoning mind is functioning and has immense powers of imagination. The children are capable of great learning in all areas of life.

Regular education misses the key opportunity of the elementary years by failing to utilize the child's unique abilities for self-formation in the earlier period. Not only educators fail to take advantage of this period of the children's great intellectual and social expansion. Parents also unwittingly neglect this time of immense opportunity in the children's formation. Because children do not insist on constant attention, as in their earlier years, parents do not focus on their needs as before. We assume that all is well because no serious problems are erupting.

In fact, in this period when children are just beginning to look outward to society with reasoning minds, parents need to be extremely alert to their children's needs. Although the children are beginning to search out their peers for companions, they are still heavily dependent upon their parents for support in every area. When parents follow their children's interests closely and make themselves available, they find that their children are full of questions about society and their place within it, of who they are and why they are here, and of the meaning of life and death. Parents who neglect this period miss the optimum time for help-ing their children build a strong base for the turbulent adolescent years to come.

Montessori education is designed to take advantage of the special characteristics given to children in the second plane of formation. Its goal goes beyond the imparting of knowledge to children. It seeks to aid children in their development as com-plete human beings. Through their exploration of the universe, the beginnings of life on earth, and of the laws and order which govern existence, the children gradually realize that everything in creation has a role to play. They are inspired to look for what it is that creates the interrelatedness of the universe and the living be-ings within it. They begin their personal search for the meaning and value in human life. In 1936, Montessori in her first lecture course relating to elementary education said, "We may say that if a culture does not raise and elevate humankind, it does not respond to the urgent need of our times. The culture that does not give light on the values of individuality and does not bring about harmony and cooperation of human beings, such a culture has a significance, as it were, of things out of date and passed away."

The Montessori teacher's specific responsibility is to aid human development through awareness of the children's needs at each stage of self-formation. Through this approach to their education, the children can pass onto each successive plane of development well prepared for the challenges ahead. In the first stage of formation, the children form their individual capacities and selfhood. They develop independence, coordinated movement, order, and language, including written language and mathematics. In the second plane, the children complete the foundation of their social selves. Through their reasoning minds and powers of imagination, they explore their universe, their community and their own place in social life.

8

△ △ △

SCENES FROM AN ELEMENTARY CLASSROOM

As we have learned, the procedures followed for the upper and lower elementary levels are essentially the same. The major difference in the two classrooms occurs as a result of the more mature state of the older children. Nine- to twelve-year-olds go into much further detail in their studies and their research, and their "going out" activities reflect a greater depth in knowledge and intensity of interests. The foundation laid in the years from six to nine makes possible the older children's advanced level of inquiry and study. Therefore, I have chosen to observe a lower elementary classroom for six- to nine-year-olds. Everything about their experience—the tone of the classroom, the demeanor of the children, and the role of the teacher—is comparable to that of an upper elementary classroom.

A MORNING VISIT

It is mid-January, several weeks after the holiday break. I have come for a visit to an elementary classroom for six- to nine-year-olds. It is nine o'clock and the children have already been in class for forty-five minutes.

I put a small chair in what I hope will be an inconspicuous spot close to one of the six large tables in the room. Each one of these tables has four to six children gathered around it. The children are working with books, papers, pencils—both colored and lead—and Montessori materials. There are also a number of low tables that stand a foot or so from the floor with several children working together at each one. Other children have put their work on small mats on the floor.

The room has a full, busy feel to it, but I doubt that one could guess that there are over thirty children here. In fact, I have been told that there are thirty-five. I scan the classroom, searching for the teacher. After a moment, I locate her seated with the children at the end of one of the larger tables. She appears to be giving a joint presentation with two of the children, one on each side of her. I search for the assistant teacher who I know is there but I cannot immediately find her.

My strongest impression of this classroom is the purposefulness of the children in their collaborative efforts. They are working constantly and they take their joint efforts seriously. At the same time, they appear relaxed and happy. They are spontaneously talking with each other and getting up at will to get some needed item or to speak to another child. Additionally, there is an air of confidence about these children. Their actions reflect respect for each other and the work in front of them—the latter no longer neatly and precisely placed, as in the primary, but with quantities of opened books, materials, notebooks, and papers casually laid out on each table and work rug.

As I settle in to observe for the morning, I begin to sense

that, for these children, relating to each other and working are a unified experience. The thought occurs to me that my primary children develop concentration through their work; these elementary children are developing themselves socially through their work.

The children's voices are low, and I can only overhear the directed conversation of the children at the table closest to me. I realize that the modulation of the children's voices is one factor that contributes to the atmosphere of respect and purposefulness that pervades this particular elementary classroom. It is not quiet like a library. There is an industrious hum of conversation going on, but it is primarily serious in tone and directed to the work that the children are doing together.

"Look at that," I hear one of the four boys next to me exclaim. "Two-hundred-pound explosive shells!" He is pointing to a picture in one of a number of opened books on the table in front of him. "Did anything blow up?" one of the boys asks. All the boys look over at the opened book which appears to be from the local library. I can see a picture of a train and notice that all the books are related to trains or to transportation generally. Two of the four boys have pads of paper in front of them and are taking notes. A third one is making an intricate pencil drawing from an illustration of a particular model of train.

The fourth boy at the table is not working on the group report (which I later learn is specifically on trains, not transportation generally). He is using graph paper to compute a math problem. He is coloring in the squares that are color-coded as in the primary classroom—red for hundreds, blue for tens, green for units—to match numbers with their place value in the decimal system. It is called the Geometric Form of Multiplication and it shows number relationships to squares and various rectangles. This boy is working on a more abstract level than earlier manipulative materials—the equivalent concrete materials in this case being the colored and Golden Bead bars of units, tens, hundreds, etc.

As this child marks his graph paper, he appears to be comfortably encompassing both experiences at the same time: his individual math work and the companionship and conversation of the other three boys as they continue on their group research. I am not certain that this is something that even the oldest children in the primary could manage. Their abilities for concentration are just not sufficiently developed. If there is more than one other child at the same table with them also doing individual work, their attention typically is drawn away from their own work.

A few feet away from me, three children are sticking pins into holes on a poster board map of Europe. The pins have tiny red labels attached with the names of countries on them. "Albania," I overhear one boy say as he reads a label to his working partners and puts it on the map. A boy and girl at a smaller table next to these children have math bead bars out which are colored to represent place value and a board with corresponding colored sections. Again the colors have the same value representation: green for units of millions, units of thousands, and simple unit, red for hundreds of thousands and simple hundreds, blue for tens of thousands and simple tens. This material is called the Checkerboard and precedes the work mentioned earlier of the Geometric Form of Multiplication.

Just beyond these children, five others have newspapers spread over a large table. I wonder what they can be doing with them. One of the children walks over to the assistant whom I now locate on the floor partially hidden behind a shelf. The boy is carrying what looks to me to be the sports section of one of the newspapers. I think to myself, These children must be following basketball scores or related sports statistics on which seven-year-olds often become fixated. This is going to be where "following their own interest" is going to break down for me personally, at least as a valid educational concept for elementary children.

The only other table on which I can see the work clearly is next to this "newspaper" table. This is a small table with only two children. Their books are standing up on end so that I can see, even across the room, that they are doing a report on jungle birds and animals—what specific aspect, however, I cannot tell. Later, these children explain to me that they are doing a report on animals and birds and their habitats. I wonder how they have picked this particular topic but I do not want to disturb them with further questions. The teacher has promised to fill in the details of my observations later in the week, and I make a note to ask her more about this particular work.

Meanwhile, the only child in the room who is obviously working alone, at least for the moment, has set up a rug not far from me. He puts a number of books on it. I can count seven. He begins to read aloud to himself from one of them. I can hear portions of phrases: "Killer whales are . . . mainly are," "fishes, squids," "attack seals and dolphins." He looks contented but I wonder why he is by himself. He is very much smaller than the other children and looks more like a five-year-old. I speculate that slower development might be a reason for his working alone, either by choice or because the other children are not including him. (I learn from the teacher later that in fact he is working on a report with a child who happens to be absent today.)

I take a moment now to survey the room as a whole again, trying to gain a sense of it overall. I write down in my notes "Work everywhere. Intent. Busy. Level of work staggering." I have in mind here the advanced reference books which the children are reading and from which they are taking notes, one of the multiplication problems that is being worked through the Geometric Form of Multiplication procedure (6,896 × 94), the geography work, and the independence with which all the children are working. Although there is no obvious directing by the adults, no one in the room, in this time at least, is idle.

I get up now to take a closer look at the work on the tables that I cannot see in detail. The children who had the pin maps out have put them away and are coloring in paper outline maps of Europe. They are writing the names of the countries in precisely formed cursive letters on each one as they finish filling it in. I realize now that when I saw them going to the assistant a few minutes earlier, they were asking her to quiz them prior to proceeding to make their maps.

The children who were using the Checkerboard with bead material earlier are now doing grammar work. They have a small red ball and black pyramid on the table, as well as cards and a box with small open compartments labeled with parts of speech. "See, the red ball is for verbs. Verbs are actions," they explain to me confidently, moving the ball around the table. "The pyramid is for nouns. Nouns are solid. That means 'stable'."

As I go past the "newspaper table," I discover, I confess to my relief, that the children are not looking at the sports section after all. They are cutting out weather maps and recording high and low temperatures across the United States. One child is flipping through a small spiral notebook. "What is that?" I ask. "My dictionary," he explains. He shows me that there are handwritten words on the alphabetized pages. "The teacher writes down words for me when I misspell them on a report," he explains.

When I get to the opposite end of the room, I find that four children are doing math problems with the Geometric Form of Multiplication. The teacher is still at the same table where she was sitting earlier, but now she is just finishing a presentation with two different children. She gets up and begins to go quietly to each group of children in the room. I can hear her say, "I am going to tell a story now. It is about early human beings." "I am going to make a presentation." "Come to the time line that is out." Her tone and manner are those of an invitation, rather than a directive. Perhaps this is why the resulting movement of the children to the time line takes place in a leisurely, almost imperceptible fashion.

The children regroup themselves along one side and at both ends of a time line that is stretched across the floor in a small open area at one side of the room. They sit two or three deep with the outside children standing and looking on over the others. I notice that they have each brought their journals as well as their spiral dictionary-spelling notebooks with them. "What time is it?" one child asks. "Ten ten," comes the reply from another. "What shall we call this presentation?" several children ask the teacher. "You can call it 'Cave Painting' or just the 'Second Time Line of Human Beings,'" she answers.

The time line is a laminated paper chart approximately thirty-six inches wide and unrolls to a length of six yards. It begins with the Upper Paleolithic period at 23,000 B.C. and covers what are labeled as the "Transitional," "Neolithic", and "Metal" periods. It ends in 2000 A.D. The early stone cultures of the Solutrean and the Magdalenian peoples and the types of vegetation—tundra, steppe, pine forest, and oak—are indicated. There are symbolic drawings, each representing a human discovery or idea, sparsely distributed throughout the time line. Two men are spearing a mammoth; close to them is a cave painting showing mammoths and rhinos; another human being is fashioning a stone; a group of humans is chasing an animal off a cliff; others are attempting to spear fish in water; several women are scraping animal skins together; a man is twisting a stick between his hands as if to strike a spark for fire; there is a hut in one place and a stockade around another area; a pulley is being used to pull a stone up over a cliff; a man is plowing with a stick while a woman weaves nearby; there are signs of domesticated animals— a dog accompanying a hunter, a pig close to a plowing scene.

The time line begins with a red line indicating the warming of the earth after the last ice age. The overall appearance of the time line is one of simplicity and deliberate limitation. The teacher begins, "This is the second time line of early humans. You remember the 'First Time Line of Human Beings' about the ice ages? This time line begins right after an ice age. What do we see?" "Tools," a child offers. "What do they use tools for?" the teacher asks. "Find things." "Find food." "Scrape the skins." "Chop down trees." Different children respond. The teacher replies, "What about homes? What could have given them the idea of shelter? What would they have seen about them?" "Caves," a child answers. "Yes, here we have a cave pictured on the time line don't we? It has a painting of a mammoth on it," the teacher comments.

All this while, different children are spontaneously offering suggestions. I am impressed that the children are so obviously uncompetitive with each other in their responses. No one is taking a dominant role or using this opportunity to attract attention to themselves. There is a quiet respect for each other's ideas. Each child appears to be thinking on his or her own, interested and deeply involved.

"People did live in caves in France," the teacher responds. "We know because we have found paintings in caves there." She holds up a book that was opened on the floor above the time line. "These are the Perigord Caves. They are from prehistory. What can you see?" "Horses," a child says. "Why animals, I wonder?" the teacher asks.

The discussion follows naturally into the drawings themselves and the idea of pictures as a language of communication. The teacher refers to the third Great Lesson, "The Story of Communication in Signs," and the children offer their thoughts: "They drew pictures to give ideas to others"; "to tell how far it was to the river"; "they carved on sticks"; "they used a mallet on rock"; "the Egyptians had hieroglyphics."

The teacher brings the children back to the cave paintings by asking, "What could they have painted with, these early humans?" The children respond, "berries," "a brush or stick," "Indians had war paint," "they used their fingers." "What was around them? I see ochre here. That is a deep yellow color," the teacher explains. "Flowers," "pollen," the children offer. "Perhaps, and they also found mineral deposits on the floor of the cave and petrified wood. They had only three colors: red, ochre, and black," the teacher continues. "They could have used mud," "coal or charcoal," the children reply. "Perhaps. Thomas you brought in petrified wood for your rock report last week. . . . What happens when you mix red and yellow?" the teacher continues. "Orange," "gold," the children respond.

"How could they get the paint on the cave walls?" the teacher asks. "With feathers," "branches," "fingers," come the replies. The teacher suggests that "they would blow paint through a tube or they could take moss or grass and dab it on." "Yeah, they could hollow a stick," a child suggests and another one says, "They could take sap off a tree." Still another goes further afield, "They could camouflage themselves." "Why would they need to?" the teacher asks. "For hunting," comes the reply. "Perhaps, but do you think that the animals could tell that there were people under the camouflage? Could they smell them?" One of the children starts to describe a television program where the photographers wore wolf skins, hoping to camouflage themselves from the wolves.

I admire the manner in which the teacher allows a tangential idea to have expression but then gently guides the conversation back to topic: "That is an interesting discussion for another day. Today let's think again about the cave paintings. Many people think cave paintings represent the earliest written language. We have allowed tourists into these caves in the past but these paintings are so valuable that we have had to limit this accessibility. People's breath has caused damage to the cave walls. So now people have made reproductions of the paintings and put them in glass cases to hang in a museum. We have also redrawn and re-painted some of the paintings and left them in the caves. These books [referring to the books which she has placed above the time line] show pictures of these preserved and restored cave paintings. There are also pictures of cave paintings in the Picture

Cards of Prehistoric People and in the Hieroglyphics Cards in the classroom. I am going to leave the time line out for a while for you to look at. I will also leave these books for you," the teacher concludes.

Some children begin to pore over the time line while others leave; still others start to write in their journals. "What time is it?" a girl who is new to the school asks. "Ten thirty," the teacher tells her but adds in a kindly tone, "You can wear a watch. That is also why we have a clock in the room. This is your responsibility." The other children are checking their own watches to write the ending time of the presentation in their journals. "You can do this, or you can go back to your work," the teacher mentions again to all the children. Some continue to look at the time line, others are on the floor poring over the books.

One boy selects a paperbound book from a nearby shelf. I recognize it as one of the little booklets written by Montessori teachers for use in the classroom. This one is entitled *The Second Book of Writing 35,000 B.C.* He is showing a page to a girl standing next to him. "That is how they made an 'A.' It is different," he explains to her.

Again I am impressed by the purposeful attitude of these children and, at the same time, their unhurried, relaxed manner. They appear to be savoring this new information to which they have just been exposed and to be exploring it further with their companions, each in his or her own way. They have time to think. That is what impresses me most, I realize. These children are thinking.

The teacher goes over to the three boys who are now back to coloring their maps of Europe. I hear her ask them if they named the countries for the assistant before beginning.

I sit down by the "weather table." One of the children explains to me, "Last night a killer earthquake hit Japan. More than fourteen hundred people died. There were thousands of injuries. A lot of people were on the bullet train that got hit from the north."[1] "This is yesterday and today's weather report," another child tells me. "The snow is moving up," he explains to the child next to him. "Yesterday it only snowed in Michigan and northern Wisconsin."

Meanwhile, the original children looking at the time line have been replaced by a different grouping of children. I marvel at the variety of interests being explored in the room at one time: math, geography, science, history, art history, and language. The teacher is now giving a math presentation to two children with a material called the Flat Bead Frame. This material allows the children to do multiplication using very large numbers. I hear her say, "How many units in twelve?" "Two." "That's right."

I notice that a number of children have not resumed the work on their tables. Instead, they are reading books. Wondering why they have not returned to their work, I go over to a child at one table, "I see that you are reading. How did you decide to do that?" "We can read anytime," he answers politely, but I sense that he wonders if I know what I am doing here. Noticing that he is reading a book about the *Titanic*, I risk another question, "How do you decide which book to read?" "We can read anything we like," he replies, equally politely, but again it is clear that he considers the answer to my question to be obvious. I move on to another table and ask a child who is reading there how he happened to select this particular book to read just now. "I don't know," he answers. "I just like fish."

Several girls at this same table are going over a history reference book together. I ask them what they are looking for. "We are writing a report on weapons," they both reply. "Swords and spears," one continues. "Violence," the other adds. "We write the names and draw the pictures. These are the Bronze Age warriors. These weapons are a thousand years old. They are very, very, very old."

I sit down to observe the room as a whole again. One boy is sweeping the floor very diligently. He keeps this up for a good ten minutes. I sense that he is using this physical work to rest and calm him. Three of the "weather children" put on their coats and go outside to check the thermometer on a nearby tree. They come back in a few minutes. The fourth child is still sitting next to me working on her report on the earthquake. She is looking at a picture of a buckled roadway. "The plate really jumped under the ground there!" she exclaims. A girl next to me is rolling up a rug with the same exacting manner and precise care as the primary children who are in the Sensitive Period for order. I am surprised as I thought elementary children no longer did this.

It occurs to me that I have just witnessed the phenomenon of the "rest," which is supposed to be granted the children after a group presentation: The relaxed exploration of the time line by several groups of children, the spontaneous selection and reading of books by others, the checking of the thermometer outside by the "weather children," the diligent sweeping and precise rolling of the rug—all are activities by various children reflecting a lower level of intellectual intensity than their work of the earlier period. Now, after this self-chosen break, the children are settling back into their work in mathematics, geography, and research reports, energized, and outwardly as intellectually productive as before.

As I leave the classroom at eleven o'clock, I find myself

wanting to ask the same question which, I know from experience, visitors to well-functioning Montessori classrooms invariably want answered: "How do the children know what to do?" The children this morning were well-occupied, learning, concentrated, interested, purposeful. Every subject area but music—for the moment—was being covered. (I learned later that on a typical day there are children playing the tone bars throughout the day.) I know the theory behind this result in the classroom and the mechanisms involved in general. They represent a process that is not difficult to understand intellectually, but it is another matter to grasp the actuality. In fact, an element of unbelief lingers in my mind about the morning. This classroom is so different from my own elementary schooling. I want to know how this particular teacher helped to facilitate this outcome with this particular group of children on this one morning. I am especially intrigued because I am aware that this teacher, who is in her mid-twenties, is a first-year teacher fresh out of the Montessori elementary training course. How does she do it?

A MEETING WITH THE ELEMENTARY TEACHER

I ask Lisa, the elementary teacher of the classroom which I have visited, the question foremost in my mind, "How do the children know what to do when they first come in the morning and throughout their seven-hour school day?"

In answer, Lisa shows me charts that she has made for each child. Each one of these charts consists of four handwritten pages and records all possible presentations. Each material or presentation has two blank columns next to it. "I mark this first column when a material or presentation is first introduced to a particular child," Lisa tells me. There is a second column then to note when the child completes the follow-up work for that material or presentation. Since follow-up work is when learning occurs, this column indicates when mastery is achieved."

Lisa continues explaining that, in addition, she updates two more charts each week. One chart has a space for each child. She lists the presentations which that child is ready for and which she wants to present when the opportunity occurs. A second chart lists each presentation that the class generally is ready for. Under each presentation she lists the children to whom she can give this presentation at this point in time. In this way, she can see at a glance all the children from whom she can form a group for a specific presentation, depending on their interest or present involvement in other work. It may be weeks before she gets to a particular presentation with a child but when she does, she marks it with a highlighter. By means of these three charts, she knows exactly what each child has done and what she might introduce to them to carry them the next step in any specific area.

I comment on the extensiveness of these charts and the amount of work involved. "It was a lot of work to set them up and I did not keep such detailed records of the children's follow-up work after presentations at first," Lisa replies. "However, when Marsilia[2] came for a visit in October, she told me to tighten the children's work. It has been working well ever since." Lisa then shows me one of the children's journals. "I write possibilities of follow-up work for any materials or presentations given to a particular child in the back of his or her journal. I tell the children that when they don't know what to do, they can look in the back of their journals for ideas," she continues. "Of course, I also talk to each child about what he or she might do in the individual meeting time so we decide this together sometimes, too. More than anything, though, the work itself just seems to capture them. And they have so much energy! I have been amazed. They are really working."

I ask Lisa to tell me more about presenting the work itself. "For example, how did you decide to present the 'Second Time Line of Human Beings' the particular morning when I visited and to choose the picture of the cave painting from among all the other illustrations on it to use as a catalyst for the children's explorations into the history of art and written language?" She explains that she gave the Great Lessons early last fall. Following this, she presented the "First Time Line of Human Beings." It was probably late November or early December. Lisa then tells me about the first time line. It spans the Pleistocene Age from 500,000 B.C. to 1 A.D. Within this time frame are the lower Paleolithic period, the Stone Age cultures and the Neolithic period. The exact dates on this time line, as the second time line which I saw, are not necessarily scientifically accurate because dates keep changing as new discoveries and methods of scientific measurement are refined. The children in the older level become very interested in the different theories of dating human beings. They want to explore questions like: "What evidence has been found and who has found it? What about individual paleontologists such as Leakey? What did they find out? What were their lives like?"

Lisa unrolls the first time line for me to see. It is nineteen feet long and thirty-six inches wide. The ice ages are depicted by icicles and the warmer periods show the glaciers melted with plants and grass growing. There are animals—woolly mammoths, rhinos, wild horses, and reindeer—depicted in the later areas. There are isolated illustrations showing people following the animals to hunt for food and an indication of a cave that they might have used for shelter. Other drawings show a person using a stone as a tool to cut down a tree and another to scrape an animal skin. Still another picture depicts a fire and a family gathered around it cooking.

Lisa explains that when the teacher first presents this time line to the children, she mentions that earlier, in the third Great Lesson, they have talked about the human capacities for thinking and loving. Now they have a 'Time Line of Human Beings' showing what might have been going on, how these early humans might have satisfied their needs for food, shelter, and clothing. In the introduction the teacher picks out a few key points based on the pictures on the time line. A few details are sufficient to arouse the children's questions. If too much is given, the children are overwhelmed and their interest shuts down. Therefore, the teacher might simply note the icicles and remind the children that in one story they talked about the fact that human beings probably originated during an ice age when it was very cold. They must have developed some way to keep themselves warm. She can remind the children of the hand chart and how they have thought about those early humans using their hands to help them meet their needs for food, shelter, and clothing.

Lisa points out the warmer period depicted on the time line when the glaciers melted and it was an easier time to live. More plants and grass could grow. It would have been a pleasanter life in such periods. All kinds of further studies can develop from each one of the illustrations given on the time line. Exactly what types of animals lived during this period? Which of those animals are still around today and which are not? The vegetation of the time was of tundra and steppe. How could the needs of those early people be satisfied in such surrounds? Did they eat all kinds of animals that were about? What kind of stone did they use for their tools? How did they work with their tools? The older children, particularly, often want to do in-depth research on the Stone Age cultures. Who were the Magdalenians? What kind of stone tools did they use? When did they include bones and antlers for tools? The curriculum is open-ended and can become as broad and as deep as the explorations of individual children.

Lisa explains that one of the most important aspects to bring to the children's attention on this particular time line is the coming together of human beings to work in groups. The children realize that from the very beginning people collaborated in their endeavors because it was more effective to do so.

It was against this background of discovery of early humans and the climate of the earth that Lisa gave the second time line presentation, which I witnessed. Lisa now explains that this was actually the second time that this time line was shown to the children. During each subsequent presentation, she picks out a particular aspect of the time line to highlight, depending upon the children to whom she is presenting and their interests. Many of these lessons are prepared in relation to "history question charts." Lisa relates that there are four of these charts which the teacher prepares during training: one each about "The Nature of the Country," "Practical Activities of the People," "The Intellectual and Spiritual Aspects of the Culture," and "Relations Within Groups and with Other Groups." The teacher chooses one question from one chart, one from another, and so on.

When dealing with prehistory the questions on the history charts are open-ended. The children become aware that they cannot be answered definitively.

The presentation that Lisa made the day that I visited her class was from the history chart entitled "The Intellectual and Spiritual Aspects of Culture." There are subsections on this chart: "What Was Their Language?" "What Was Their Education Like and How Advanced Was Their Learning?" "What Was Their Art Like?" "What Were Their Ideas About Life and Death?" "Who if Anyone Was Their Spiritual Leader?" "What Concept of Justice Did They Have?" The question Lisa selected from among these suggestions was "What Was Their Art Like?"

There are many other charts leading from the "Second Time Line of Human Beings" that relate to the various areas depicted: an exploration of agriculture, for example, which could lead to a study of civilizations and the formation of towns or of vegetation and its spread through the world. Again supportive materials for such studies are made by the teacher during the training course.

Lisa shows me one chart, for example, that illustrates the spread of vegetation in the various climate zones: torrid, temperate, and frigid. She explains that the children have established a background of knowledge prior to their introduction to this chart through their studies of the needs of the plant and the leaf. These earlier studies were introduced to the children through Biology Cards and Booklets. The children are also aware of the work of water on earth and the effects of the cycle of water through follow-up group studies after the first and second Great Lessons.

The vegetation chart Lisa shows me has yellow areas to depict deserts. Lisa relates that a follow-up presentation from this part of the chart could include the clever way that plants, such as the cactus, store water. Dark green areas represent the forests. Here the leaves need a way to get rid of their water, so they grow up to the sunlight for vaporization. In one accompanying experiment, the teacher can put a plastic bag over a plant illustrating the condensation and the formation of carbon dioxide that occurs in a rain forest. In torrid areas that are less wet than a rain forest, there are only grasses and trees with fewer leaves. In the temperate zones there are oaks and maples, and in the winter these trees lose their leaves. This is a brown area on the chart. Finally, the frigid zones are white. The trees grow to a great height and the leaves are needles which have very small surfaces and therefore do not readily lose water. At the extreme of this zone where there is sunlight for only a few hours, there are only lichens.

Fascination with this adjustment of vegetation to the degree of temperature and available water and light is natural to young children when they have been exposed to live plants and animals in their early years. This is a major reason for the inclusion of plants and animals in Montessori primary classrooms.

From the "Spread of Vegetation" charts, Lisa explains that the children can discover the correlation of human and animal populations and habitats with plant growth. This exploration leads to a discovery of the adjustment of peoples to their climatic zones. The charts identify the Inuits, African-Americans, Native Americans, and Caucasians. Each of these charts depicts samples of buildings for particular climates. When using these charts, the teacher can give examples of appropriate clothing and demonstrate other ways in which human beings meet their fundamental needs in particular climatic zones. The key point is to help children understand that differences in peoples are generally due to variations in environments. It is these differences in both climates and peoples which arouse the children's interest in further study.

Lisa says that a few basic reference books[3] are suggested in the training course to aid the teacher: from the Cambridge Introduction to World History series, *The Coming of Civilization* and *People Become Civilized*, both by Trevor Cairns and *The Earliest Farmers and the First Cities* by Charles Higham. The teacher has to resist the temptation to create her own curriculum on topics that capture her attention from these texts, however. Her personal interests and knowledge are of little use to the children. She serves as a catalyst to the children's own explorations, not as an authority on specific subject matter.

At the end of our discussion together, Lisa asks me, "Can I tell you what really excites me about Montessori? It is because it is part of life. Everything connects. Each area leads to the other both for me and for the children. Whatever we touch on in class is reflected in the outside world." Lisa then goes on to tell me that the day after my visit to class, she was giving a science presentation on flower dissection with a group of children. They were discussing how the stem is like a tube through which water is carried from the roots to the leaf. Suddenly, one child said, "Oh, so you mean they could have blown paint through this?" Lisa knew immediately who "they" referred to, as undoubtedly the other children did who were present for the cave painting story.

That same night watching the news on television, Lisa

learned that an exciting new discovery of caves used by early humans had just been made in the Ardeche River Canyon near the town of Valon Pont-d'Arc, two hundred sixty miles south of Paris. Searchers came upon cave walls with more than three hundred paintings of woolly-haired rhinos, bears, hyenas, panthers, and other animals standing, galloping, and fighting. Minerals on the cave floor—iron oxide and manganese—had been used for paint. Explorers found the bones of hibernating bears and hearth flints and torches used by humans.

A day or so after this, Lisa was reading book three, *The Voyage of the "Dawn Treader,"* from *The Chronicles of Narnia* by C. S. Lewis, to the children at lunchtime. In chapter ten, entitled the "Magician's Book," there was an illustration of manuscripts of the Middle Ages and a description of the magnificent gold and blue calligraphy on parchment done by the monks. The children were fascinated by the artistry of this writing and related it to the samples of cave painting and medieval writing which they found in the reference book left out for them above the second time line a few days earlier.

The explanations that Lisa has given me about her record keeping and the work proceeding from a presentation help me to understand the enthusiasm and energy of the children for their work. Now I want to know more about the daily schedule and practical routines of this particular elementary classroom. I ask Lisa if the children have a group presentation, such as the one I saw on the "Second Time Line of Human Beings," every day in the morning or afternoon, or perhaps every few days. "Oh, no!" she answers. "Not nearly that often. The schedule is always flexible, depending on the children's responses, but the average span of time between group presentations, such as you witnessed, is

probably no more than once every two weeks or so." This information helps me to understand how a three-hour uninterrupted
work cycle can be maintained on a consistent basis.

I ask about the schedule of the day in terms of lunch, clean
up, and dismissal. Lisa tells me that at 11:30 the children gather
together. This is their time for discussing anything that needs to
be covered by the group as a whole: routines in the classroom,
who has chosen specific clean-up jobs, relationships among the
children, "going out" activities, sometimes the children have a report that they want to share, sometimes Lisa wants to cover some
aspect of their work that she feels needs amplification, and so
forth. At the end of this group time, the children come one by
one to show their journal to Lisa and to get their basket for
lunch. In this school, the children bring their own lunch to
school. Lunch is used as an educational opportunity through
which both social manners and good nutritional habits are encouraged. The children pack their own lunches with healthy
foods and cloth place mats, napkins, flatware, ceramic plates, and
glassware. Taking time to set their places properly and later to
wash their own dishes along with their companions helps to
make eating lunch a pleasant social experience and time of
sharing.

Lisa's mentioning of the journals reminds me that I want to
know more about the spelling-dictionary notebooks that the
children carry with them. "I am checking their spelling all the
time in their work," she explains. "When I see recurring mistakes
such as 'sum' for 'some,' for example, I might ask the children to
correct their work right away. Otherwise, I will write the word
correctly in their dictionary notebook for their own follow-
through later. I also have a basket of perhaps fifty spelling cards

for which everyone is responsible. They practice by themselves, usually by giving dictation to each other."

"As individual children finish lunch," Lisa continues, "they get a book to read by themselves or sometimes one child reads to another. The children cannot return to work because the tables are in use by the remaining children. By 12:30 or so all the children are finished and they gather as a group again while I read to them for perhaps fifteen or twenty minutes. During this time, two of the children sweep the room and two others make certain all the tables are clean and ready for work again."

Lisa explains that the only variation in this schedule occurs on Friday afternoons. She saves this time for her meetings with individual children.[4] Since she has thirty-five children, I realize that she cannot comfortably see them all in one afternoon. "That's right," Lisa replies. "I have divided the children in half so I see each one every two weeks. It seems to be working out well for them. There are a few exceptions and I do still meet with those children weekly. Actually, there are three of them at this point in time." I still wonder if she does not feel pressured, trying to meet with twenty children on an individual basis in a period of two and one-half hours. Lisa tells me that it works because she does not allow any interruptions during this time. Her assistant is a help in this, although she believes that if she did not have her, the children would manage on their own for this period of time.

At the close of our meeting, I remember one more question. Parents of my six-year-old children are often concerned about how their children will fare in the social freedom of the Montessori elementary classroom. They ask me how the elementary teacher arranges the groups in which the children are to work. I always tell them that the teacher does not do this because the children need to be in charge of their own social experiences. It is only in this way that they can learn from them what is necessary to prepare themselves for their lives as adults. It is a good textbook answer, but I know that my parents are looking for reassurance that their particular child will not be placed in a situation that he or she is not equipped to handle.

I ask Lisa how the groupings of children work out in practice in this elementary classroom. Do they vary their companions sufficiently? Do they mix ages? Interests? Abilities? Best friends? Lisa replies that with this particular class, children have been remarkable in choosing their companions well and in a very natural and easy-going way. She does say, however, that on rare occasions, she has separated children. Last week, for example, she felt that two children were not getting much accomplished together and several times she had spoken to them about silly behavior. After observing the situation for a day or so, she separated the children. She called their parents to explain her decision, so that they could understand her actions and add their support.

Lisa also tells me that when children are new to the classroom, they sometimes come to her and ask with whom they might work. Because, as is typical of boys and girls at this age, the children work more often with those of their own sex, she usually mentions someone of the opposite sex. Other than these two sets of circumstances, she has not found it necessary to intervene in the children's working relationships.

It occurs to me that, as in the primary classroom, it is the emphasis on work that defuses any tension between the children. In the primary level, this work is carried out by the children acting individually. In the elementary class, it is work undertaken with others.

As I leave, I ask Lisa if I can visit her class on two more occasions. I want to observe the children arriving in the morning and selecting their work, and I want to see the final moments of the afternoon as the children finish their work and prepare the classroom for the following day.

THE BEGINNING OF A CLASSROOM DAY

Because it is five minutes before the official start of the school day, I am surprised that ten children are here and at work when I enter the classroom. There is also a good deal of work on tables and rugs that was obviously left out from the day before. I count seven rugs holding books, papers, and reports in progress, in addition to several more with paper maps of the United States and South America being constructed by the children. Lisa is giving a lesson on grammar with the Grammar Boxes to two children. Several children are writing in their journals and one boy is going through a red folder box which is on the floor next to one of the shelves. "I am getting my report out to work on," he explains to me. There is already a steady quiet hum of activity in the room.

I go by a table to get a closer look at the work several children are doing. A girl has an atlas and paper maps of the United States, Africa, Australia, Europe, and Asia in front of her. The maps have only the rivers and lakes printed on them. She has outlined some of these with a blue pencil and written their names. "We are looking up their names in this atlas," she tells me. A boy at this table is working on a report on prairie dogs. "How did you get the idea to do a report on prairie dogs?" I ask. "It is from the Story Material Box. It has picture cards of animals and things written about them," he responds. "It has birds"—

"hummingbirds," a child who has just sat down offers—"sala-manders, a golden eagle, and a snake," he continues. "A rattle-snake," the second child clarifies again and adds, "these are all animals that are native to Illinois."

I discover from Lisa later that this story material on animals is used in the same way as the time lines are. Both help the children to get involved in research. The "Time Lines of Human Beings" focus on the needs of humans and the different ways in which they meet their needs. There is a box of story material that has separate strips with suggested questions to research: in which element does this animal live—water, air or land? How does it eat—carnivorous, herbivorous, and omnivorous? How does it re-produce—oviparous (eggs), viviparous (born alive), or ovovivipa-rous? How does it move—walk, creep, flight, swim? And finally, how does it care for its offspring—provides food, suckle, or does nothing? Research stimulated by the two boxes of story material give the children an informational base for the classification of animals and an in-depth study of the animal kingdom which they carry out in the nine-to-twelve class. A correlation of this zoological material for the study of plants is provided in boxes of Botanical Cards and Booklets. Similarly, there is a file of scientific experiments with questions to be answered, which follow from the Great Lessons and Key Lessons. Using command cards the children carry out their own experiments and write up what they have observed. They may use microscopes on their own, but if a hot plate or flame is needed, the assistant helps to set it up. Again, if chemicals are required for an experiment, the assistant is always present.

A number of children are steadily entering the room now, doing so in a natural but unobtrusive way. They seem almost businesslike as they take off their coats and hang them on hangers in the small entranceway to the classroom that doubles as a cloakroom. Each child comes to Lisa to shake hands, then each one gets out his or her journal and writes the date, time, and work begun. I overhear several children say to each other, "What shall we do today?" For the most part, however, the children seem to be continuing with work already begun in the day or days before. I note that a number of the children have formed into different groups from my last visit.

"Did you know that turtles lay sixty to two hundred eggs?" a boy who got his report from the folder box asks me. He has a clipboard with lined paper on it and is starting to write this information down as he talks to me. I notice several children working on the Large Bead Frame. This is a transitional material that is first introduced in the primary class. The children can work addition, multiplication, and subtraction problems with it. In the primary level, the children use it individually. Here each child is writing the problem and answer on his or her own sheet of paper, but the children are working the answers out together on the single Large Bead Frame. At another table, I again see children working with a transitional math material. This time it is the Division with Racks and Tubes. Again, this is a material used individually in the primary classroom, and here two boys are working with it together. They are having a disagreement as to how to proceed. One boy gets up to ask Lisa which one of them is right. He seems very convinced that he is, and somewhat irritated with his companion for not realizing this. I am impressed, however, with the mature way in which both boys handle this disagreement. When Lisa comes to explain that the boy who came to get her is in fact correct, both children continue with their work in a matter-of-fact manner as if no problem had occurred.

I follow Lisa back to the table where she is continuing her grammar presentation. There is a sentence on a card which she asks the children to read: "Do not look this word up in the dictionary but look it up in the encyclopedia." As she goes on with the lesson, I am aware that she is continually asking the children to use their own minds: which words are the nouns, which ones are the articles, which the verbs, and so forth. The children put the symbols, which they learned in the Function of Word Exercises (for each part of speech) in primary above the proper words. There is a quiet animation in Lisa's voice as she asks, "Which word takes the place of the noun? What is 'it' referring back to?" After all words are symbolized, she continues, "Now we are going to play a little game."

At this point, I turn to a boy at the same table working on a report on cave painting. He has several books from his home and from the library. He asks Lisa about something in one of them. "Let me finish this sentence then I will talk to you more about it," she answers. He gets up then and goes across the room to talk to a child at another table. I notice that it is 8:55 and that the pleasant noise level in the room continues. The children are all talking with each other, which adds to the "at ease" feeling of the room; but they are speaking in low, conversational tones. One child comes up to another and I hear him say, "Do you like my dog?" I ask to see his drawing, too. It is an elaborate and amazingly accurate free-hand representation of a dog with its parts labeled. Both boys then proceed to read together the accompanying report which it illustrates, "The body parts of the dog are the muzzle, crest, neck, croup or rump, cheek, jaw, withers, line or flank, thigh, hock, joint, brisket, elbow, stifle [which they pronounce 'steefle'], pad, forearm, and pastern." The drawing is so perfect, yet clearly not traced, that I ask how old this boy is. "Seven," he answers. "My birthday is August 19."

The child researching cave painting is back now and Lisa answers the question. It had something to do with how old the painting is. Lisa says that the man who has written the book is a famous painter of today who thinks that these cave people painted better than he does. He has written that no one knows how old these cave paintings are. "They probably know now," the child replies. Lisa then shows him how to look on the title page to see when the book was first published and for subsequent printings. "You mean that I could get ideas from this to talk about how old they are?" he asks. "Yes, absolutely," Lisa responds. "That is what everyone does. Find out what it says and then put it in your own words." As Lisa goes on with her grammar lesson, I ask this child how old he is and when he moved from the primary class. "I am six," he answers. "I came in here just after Christmas" (a month ago). I notice that he has finished quite a few pages on his report already and I ask if he minds if I read it. The page on top is titled, "How they made their Paint," and he has written, "They used egg white or plant juice to make a kind of paint which they put on the walls with brushes made of animal fur or feathers and pads of moss or leaves." The illustration which he has given it is of a brush fashioned with bone and animal fur. The parts are labeled.

I look back to the earlier pages. The first page is entitled "hunters prey" and says, "Cave paintings some 20,000 years old often show animals that were hunted at the time, like this deer in dordogne, france." The second one has the title, "Subtle tones" and he has written, "Most painted figures were simple outlines, like this charcoal sketch of a horse on the walls of a cave at niaux in the french pyrenees, in some cases figures were filled in either wholly or partly." Both these first two pages are illustrated with amazingly accurate drawings of cave paintings. The next page has a picture from the newspaper for its illustration and I recognize that it is from an article on the new cave discoveries that Lisa discussed with me a few days ago. He has titled this page, "The New Painting," and it reads, "20,000 years ago in the canyon of the ardeche river, 300 paintings of woolly haired rhinos, bears, oxen, goats, panthers, owls and hyenas were painted, now they are found. Some of the animals are shown in groups, standing or galloping. Some rhinos are fighting."

I notice that this boy's journal is next to him and I ask if I may look at it, too. "Yes," he replies and goes right on with his work. The entry for today so far says "January 17 8:40 report on cave painting." I turn back to yesterday's page: "January 16 9:04 report on cave painting; 10:20 rotation of the earth; 10:40 geometrical multiplication." Because this day is incomplete, I turn back a few pages for another sample.

As I looked over his entries on other days, I note that they usually consist of between three and five items a day.

"I still remember the definite and the indefinite article," a child in the grammar lesson says next to me. The enthusiasm in her voice jars me back to the moment and a consciousness of the class as a whole. As I look at the environment, the maturity of everyone strikes me. There is nothing that might invite silly behavior. Perhaps that helps to account for the purposeful behavior of these children. They are involved, yet comfortably so. They are not paying the least attention to me, and I can understand why parents are always asking to observe for a day, thinking that they are not disturbing the children in any way. I know that it is not the same to have more adults in the class, however, and that I should leave. More than one teacher and one assistant in the classroom can interfere with the children's development of independence and self-direction, and constant observation by visitors interferes with the spontaneity of the children's responses.

I stop to look at the work of several children on my way out. Two children are reading a booklet of the parts of the leaf, "A leaf is a laminar expansion of the plant which grows from the stem. It is veined and usually green in color." "We are going to

JANUARY 10	8:50	GEOMETRICAL MULTIPLICATION	9:10
	9:11	PIN MAP	9:35
	9:35	COLOR IN A MAP	10:10
	9:50	TIME LINE (*I notice some time crossover here and wonder if he did go to a presentation and then back to his map.*)	10:00
	10:34	TONE BARS (*a musical instrument in the classroom*)	10:40
	10:50	READ A BOOK (*Here he obviously encompassed lunchtime.*)	1:14
		GEOMETRICAL MULTIPLICATION	3:15

make a booklet," they tell me. Because one of my purposes in observing the children early in the morning is to understand better their specific choices for work, I ask them how they decided to choose this work. They both looked puzzled and answered, "I don't know."

A boy next to them is multiplying two numbers together with the Geometric Form of Multiplication. He has taped several pieces of graph paper together. I ask him to read his problem to me. He smiles up at me, showing that two front teeth are missing, and reads, "23 trillion, 454 billion, 325 million, 532 thousand, 322 times 654 thousand, 622." "How did you choose that problem?" I ask in surprise. "I made it up," he answers and gives me another big grin.

At the next table, a boy is working on suffixes. He has written, "teach, teacher, teaching, electric, electrician, electricity." I ask him what caused him to choose this particular work today. He also replies, "I don't know." When I ask him if he looked in the back of his journal for ideas, he says, "No, I was doing it yesterday at three." Intrigued now with the fact that the children do not seem to be aware of conscious choice in their work, I ask two girls next to him who are working with weights on a scale how they happened to choose this material. "Were you doing it yesterday?" "No," they both answer. Then one says, "It's like 'challenger.' I don't know how we decided to do it." Finally, as if she has been thinking hard about it, the other girl answers, "We had a lesson on it yesterday." "There, they're even," I hear one girl say as I move on. "No, too heavy," the other replies.

On my way to Lisa to say good-bye and to thank her, I go by the white board on the wall that serves the function of a chalkboard for the class. I notice that Lisa has written there what looks like ideas for the kinds of information to include in reports. I ask two children who are close by if this is something that the teacher wrote on the board to give them suggestions for work. "No, we did it," they say. As I leave, I ask Lisa about the information on the board. She tells me that at group time before lunch yesterday, she went over the type of information that might be pertinent for reports. She felt that some children needed guidance in staying with relevant ideas. One child had written a report on Greece, for example, and had written, "The shortest person in Greece is . . . the tallest person is . . ." She suspected that he made up the numbers, which she could not recall. At group time, she gave some humorous examples of trivia to the children, and they had a discussion about what might be important for people to know about a topic or person. The children had come up with all the ideas, and she had written them on the board for them to refer to for a day or so. I look back at the board and am amazed by the inclusiveness of the four columns there. Under "Place" is listed "population of people, size, square footage, native birds and animals, geography and landscape, waterways, plants and trees, climate and weather, natural resource, daily life, clothing and food, cities including capitals, history, art, language, money." Under the column for "Person" the suggestions read "dates of life, place lived, reasons for fame, accomplishments, what their life was like, what life was like at the time when they lived, how they died, family." The next column lists "Events": "name, date, what it was about, how it started and ended, place, people involved, leader at the time and important details." The last column is for "Animals" and lists "name, habitat, weight, heights, size, what they eat, where they live in the world, how many in the world, endangered?, body parts and skeleton, color, body covering, their young, species—vertebrate or invertebrate, speed, sounds they make."

I think about the fact that this is not a meaningless list for the children precisely because they have composed it themselves. They were having a problem in their research; their teacher has appealed to their own resources to solve the difficulty. Because these are elementary children, even though the problem is one of individual perception, the solution is sought in synergistic effort.

THE END OF THE CLASSROOM DAY

I come in the classroom at 3:10 and am surprised to see that there are no signs that the end of the day is nearly at hand. There is a good deal of work to do to clean up the room for the next day, and I would have expected that the children would have begun. Instead, the children are still hard at work, just as I left them earlier in the morning. The child who was researching rivers and lakes for her maps is still at it. "Did you work on this all day?" I ask. "Yes," she answers and smiles at me. Two children are working with a Grammar Box. "Which box is this?" I question. "Box Eight," they answer. "How did you decide to work with this particular one?" "I don't know," they respond with the same puzzled look of the children this morning. Several children are working on leaf booklets, others on reports on birds. Still others have the Checkerboard and the Division with Racks and Tubes out.

I stop by several children who are working on a material that I have not seen. "This is the Area Material," one child tells me. He shows me a series of geometric shapes with grids of small squares on them. He demonstrates how by fitting two right-angled triangles, for example, into a rectangle, then counting the squares of vertical and horizontal lines, he can find their base and height. "Base times height. That equals the area," he says confidently. A child next to him holds a rock with a fossil up for me to see. "I found this digging in my driveway this summer," he explains. "I was thinking if I do a report on it." Two children across the table have the Bead Bars out. They have 3 five bars out and 5 three bars in front of them. "Oh, opposites," one says. "Oh, look, the same answer!"

Gradually, in the space of time since I entered the room, I sense an energy build up in the children, as if they are getting ready for a change. There is a feeling of anticipation but without the excitement that I associate with children getting out of school in more traditional settings. There is a directed, purposeful quality to these children as if they are gearing up for a new endeavor or preparing for a trip. I notice the assistant starting to go to individual groups of children and tell them that it is time to "straighten up." It is 3:20. One of the children is also going around the room saying, "It's time to clean up now." He has a posterboard chart in his hand with clothespins attached to it. He shows me that each clothespin has a child's name on it and is clipped to a specific job designated on the chart. "I am the Inspector today," he explains. "I check all the jobs and the shelves." He turns back to the task at hand. "Did you get your job inspected?" he says in a businesslike manner to a nearby child. A boy walks past me. "We all help out," he offers over his shoulder to me, "because people need help."

The classroom is a veritable beehive of activity. Children have dusters and are going over shelves. Others have dust pans and brooms and are sweeping the floor. Some are putting chairs up on tables. One boy is industriously spraying and wiping the white board clean. A child goes past me with a watering can, explaining as she does so, "This is the time of day when everyone does their jobs. I'm watering the plants."

Everyone is busy but there is no pandemonium. In particular, there is none of the silliness which primary children can fall into when they have a feather duster or dust mop in their hands. These older children work rapidly to accomplish a purpose and have the look of those who control their own destiny, who know where they are going and how they are going to get there. I am accustomed to the much slower, deliberate pace of the younger children; it is like witnessing a whirlwind of activity. In a matter of a few minutes, the room is straightened, inspected, and the children are waiting with their coats on. Those who are acting as "runners" for the day begin to call individual children outside for their rides home. Afterwards I realize that what is so remarkable about this whole process is that the children are so completely in charge of their own dismissal. Shaking hands with each individual child appears to be the limit of the teacher's involvement.

As I turn to take a last look at this well designed classroom with its carefully laid-out shelves and beautifully constructed materials, I think to myself that it is no wonder this all works so well. The teacher has everything she needs at her fingertips: all the materials with which to teach, not facts given to the children to memorize but tools and starting points for the children's own explorations. If the teacher has the ability to organize and a sincere respect for and interest in children and knowledge, there is no limit to the possibilities for a meaningful education in a Montessori elementary classroom.

9
△ △ △

THE PLANES OF ADULTHOOD

To my knowledge, Montessori is unique among educators in that she included all the formative years from birth to adulthood in a comprehensive educational plan. We have discussed her plan of education for the years from birth to age twelve. Montessori had just completed her program for the elementary child at her death, in 1952, at age eighty-two. She was never able to turn her full attention to the last half of the formative stage, the two planes of adulthood, from twelve to eighteen years and eighteen to twenty-four years.

Although Montessori was unable to work out in detail educational designs for the third and fourth planes, she had developed a theoretical framework for them by the late 1930s. Its principles were presented in lectures which were given as part of Montessori's International Training Courses, in England and Holland, from 1936 to 1939.[1] In part, Montessori outlined her ideas for the adolescent in response to requests by Dutch parents wishing to continue their children's Montessori education into the secondary-school years. She acted as an adviser to several high schools that are still in operation today.

Because she was not involved on a daily basis, Montessori wanted to distinguish these Dutch schools of secondary education from the Children's Houses and Montessori Elementary Schools to which she was devoting herself full-time and for which she felt responsible. She, therefore, agreed to help with the new high schools to the extent possible but asked that they not be called "Montessori" schools. She believed that her own expertise should not be the deciding factor in the practical details of the secondary educational plan. She stated that the continuation of her method would have to come from the young persons themselves and direct experience with them, just as had her educational plans at the primary and elementary levels.

By 1978, a group of American parents, following the Dutch precedent, became interested in continuing Montessori education for their adolescent children. By 1994, there were more than one hundred adolescent programs at Montessori schools in the United States, and their number grows yearly. To date, most of them are middle-school programs, for students twelve to fifteen years old, with graduates entering regular high schools at the ninth or tenth grades. In developing these pioneering programs, teachers are attempting to follow Montessori's advice, to observe their students within the framework of her philosophical ideas and to adjust their approach to meet the needs of the students, as they become apparent.

Montessori regarded adolescence as a period of great vulnerability. She likened the first three years of this period of transition to adulthood, the years from twelve to fifteen, to the first three years of life from birth to age three. The infant is in a totally vulnerable state and requires careful attention and devotion on the part of adults. A new being is in creation, a child. In this second period also, great weakness is apparent, and very special consideration must be given. Again, a new creation is taking place, this time, an adult.

As in the early stage of childhood, adolescence is a period of self-construction. During these years, the adolescent is introverted and self-conscious. At the same time, he or she is also seeking to join society as an adult member. There is, therefore, an interest in social organization and other peoples of the world. Montessori referred to this psychological characteristic as "an abstract social sentiment for humankind" in which the adolescent seeks to "understand people's behavior in the world as a whole, including the past." The adolescent wishes to discover both the self and society, in order to take his or her place in the adult world as a contributing member. According to Montessori, the goal of this exploration is the creation of "the socially conscious individual."

In the first plane of formation, children are "sensorial explorers"; in the second, they are "reasoning explorers." Now, in the third plane, they become "humanistic explorers," interested in the quality of society for themselves and for other peoples of the world. In order to educate the youngest children in the means for living responsibly within a community of others, Montessori developed the exercises of "grace and courtesy." The elementary children continued this process of social awareness and the formation of social skills through freedom for social exploration, both within the classroom and in the local community. At the secondary level, young persons develop a respect for and commitment to a code of civility for their lives as adult citizens within society at large. According to Montessori, behavior befitting a citizen can best be accomplished through active and full participation in the society during the adolescent years.

In addition, Montessori believed that adolescents have an

equal need for "calm and solitude," if they are to make sense of the self and the world. They are filled with "doubts, hesitations, emotions, discouragements." They are very sensitive, embarrass easily, and lack confidence. Their sensitivity is "sometimes accompanied by a lack of discipline and revolt against authority if the latter lacks sympathy and understanding." They have a great "need for the strengthening of self-confidence." They have difficulty concentrating and are easily distracted, making it difficult for them to assimilate study as before.[2]

At the same time, adolescents are impressive intellectually. They want to discuss abstract ideas and reason through to conclusions based on evidence. They are interested in discussing moral and spiritual issues, the purpose of life and the meaning of death. They like to debate what the author of a book is really saying, or an artist truly intending through his painting, or a composer expressing through her music. They want to explore what others are thinking and feeling and are perceptive about their strengths and weaknesses.

Montessori had a deep faith in the benefits of academic knowledge and intellectual study. In spite of the adolescent's diminished capacity to concentrate, she believed that, provided the right methods were employed, it was important "to enlarge and not reduce the field of knowledge . . . education must be very broad and very complete—not only for those who are able to go on to intellectual professions but for all human beings who live in a time characterized by the progress of science and its applications."[3] As for study itself, she believed that it answers a "need of the intelligence" and, as such, does not cause "mental fatigue" but rather regenerates and strengthens "the development of the mind."[4]

Montessori stated that adolescents have a great need for creative expression. Their creative urges represent not so much artistic feelings, as a means for self-expression and self-discovery. Because they lack confidence, they need encouragement in their creative expression. She noted that the young child's drive for independence is extended at the third plane into two new areas. The desire to help others, which was just beginning to surface at the end of the elementary years, now expands into a need to make a "direct contribution to society and have it recognized." In addition, the adolescent has a "desire to become financially independent."[5]

Adolescents need encouragement in their efforts to achieve this extended independence. They look for support in two places: in a community of peers and, when given the opportunity, in an adult friend. Montessori believed that, properly constituted, the school is the natural place to meet both of these needs.

The overriding interest of adolescents is an exploration of reality. They want this discovery to include both the natural world and the world of human organization: commerce, trade, production, and economic exchange. In the natural world, they want to test themselves, to experience what they can do and what they can be.[6] Montessori believed that the success of this exploration is the key to human social progress. She refers to the adolescents' abilities to form themselves into socially responsible personalities as a "mystery"—a mystery within which "the innermost calling of humankind is found."[7]

Montessori's emphasis on the development of personality is consistent throughout the stages of human development. Montessori refers to the full development of the younger child's personality as a process of "normalization." At this third plane of development, Montessori uses the term "valorization" of the personality. Valor is a derivative of the Latin word *valere*—to be strong or worthy. It is in this sense of discovering and developing one's own worthiness and strength that Montessori considers the "valorization of personality" as the goal of the third plane.

The necessity for self-esteem is a concept much in vogue among educators, psychologists, and parents today. Montessori was not referring to self-worth, however, as an ideal based on the dignity of all human life, important as that concept is, but as a practical notion grounded in the individual's profound sense of real accomplishment. Montessori stated that "The whole life of the adolescent should be organized in such a way that it will enable him or her, when the time comes, to make a triumphal entry into social life, not entering it debilitated, isolated, or humiliated, but with head high, sure of himself or herself. Success in life depends on a self-confidence born of a true knowledge of one's own capacities, combined with the many-sided powers of adaptation; in fact, on what we have called valorization of the personality." And how is this "valorization of the personality" to be achieved? According to Montessori, as in the process of normalization for the younger child, it can only come about through work and direct experiences of the environment.[8]

The challenge of the educator at the third plane of development is to devise a plan of education that combines intellectual study and discovery with real life situations—both in nature and in society. In Montessori's plan for adolescents, academic studies are to be guided by teachers trained in secondary education, but they are to follow the principles established at the elementary level. In other words, subjects are to be interlinked rather than divided into categories. In addition, students are to be encouraged to follow their own interests. Although "free choice" is the goal, the teacher, as before, serves as a necessary guide to ensure that the students "do not waste their time and energy in aimless activity."[9] He or she is to be certain that all areas of study are covered and that academic standards for further schooling or college preparation are met. In keeping with the adolescent's more developed intellectual powers and interest in discussion and debate, seminar classes are the most suitable format.

Montessori mentions six areas as the foundation of the academic program for the adolescent: mathematics, science, language, history, creative and performing arts, and independent study. She was unusual in her early recognition of the need for emphasis on mathematics for all students. Speaking in the late 1930s, she defined human intelligence as "no longer a natural intelligence but a mathematical intelligence. . . . In our time, a mind without mathematical culture is comparable to that of a person ignorant of the alphabet at the time when literary culture came to the forefront." To develop understanding in mathematics, education must continue to connect the hand and the mind. Montessori believed that because of the "vital importance of mathematics . . . special methods" must "render the individual concepts clear and understandable by the help of concrete examples."

In the sciences, the adolescent is "to study the earth and living nature . . . geology [with emphasis on prehistoric ages], biology, botany, zoology, physiology, astronomy and comparative anatomy." There is to be an emphasis on the young person's own "practical experiments" and on an understanding of the relationship of science "to human progress and the building of civilization through the physical, chemical and other sciences."

Montessori stated that "the basis of all civilizations rests on the products of the earth." Because the adolescent seeks an understanding of civilization and working society, Montessori called her adolescent program, *Erdkinder*, or "children of the earth." This emphasis on the connection of science and human invention at the secondary level, ensures that the young person's comprehension of the interdependence of the natural world and human life, which was established in the elementary class, continues.

Montessori was particularly concerned that adolescents develop an understanding of human technology as represented by machines and the power that those machines engender. She believed that human beings assume "heavy responsibilities . . . in regard to the whole of humanity from the moment that their power rises above that of their nature proper." To help adolescents gain a degree of control and independence in regard to machines and their uses, Montessori proposed that the *Erdkinder* should include a "museum of machines." The museum would serve as an exhibit and workshop where students could learn to use and repair the machines of daily life. She listed the inventions of her day: microscopes, projectors, radios, typewriters, automobiles, and household appliances. Today it would be logical to include television sets, computers, fax machines, cellular telephones, and so forth. A comprehension of nuclear power and its potential for positive and destructive uses would also be important to Montessori's concepts of human responsibility and the interrelationship of technology and the sciences.

Montessori regarded "the development of language" as "a part of the personality itself." She considered words as "the natural means to express an idea and consequently to establish understanding between human beings." An ability to communicate with others effectively is a natural outcome of the children's freedom to talk at will with each other in Montessori classrooms at every age level. In addition to this free communication, the study of literature, advanced grammar and composition, as well as the origin and history of words, is continued. Montessori believed that "whereas formerly a single language sufficed," now "it is essential to teach different languages." Montessori did not specify the type or number of languages to be studied. She herself was proficient in Italian, French, Dutch and, to a lesser extent, Spanish and English. It is clear that she considered it of vital importance to be able to communicate with others in their native language.

In the study of history, Montessori suggested that the focus should not be "wars and conquests," as it often is in the study of human civilizations; rather, it should be the changes in the daily lives of people that are caused by "human exploration and inventions," geographical changes, and variations in climate. These circumstances result in the intermingling of peoples and the cross-culturalization of races and societies. Attitudes, customs, religions, and social behavior of human beings are all thereby affected.

Montessori outlined an extensive program in the creative and performing arts for the *Erdkinder*. This emphasis on the arts meets the needs of adolescents and is a natural culmination of the self-expression and creativity encouraged in all earlier Montessori environments. In music, Montessori suggested "the study of composers and their periods and the study of instruments both in solo and orchestral performance." In dramatic art, she mentioned "diction, elocution, dramatic or poetic representations, the art of expressing oneself logically and reasonably in discussion and debate, and the ability to give oral readings and lecture presentations." For studio art, Montessori emphasized "drawing, sculpting and painting."

To further develop their capacities for research which were begun at the elementary level, adolescents are to undertake an independent study in an area of particular interest to them. The topic chosen should have "the possibility of delving into it in sufficient depth as to gain a total comprehension of it." It follows that all or a major portion of the students' time would be occupied for at least a semester, possibly two, in this project. Montessori suggested that it would be particularly beneficial if adolescents completed an in-depth study of their own country: "its constitution, its laws, its particular characteristics, and its moral character." Other areas that might be chosen would naturally reflect the "seeds of interest," which were presented at the elementary level and which represented every field of knowledge.[10]

The schedule of academic studies is to be flexible with large blocks of uninterrupted time. The vulnerability of early adolescence suggests that students do best when not pressured and given time to develop their thoughts. Montessori believed that variation in schedule is the best way to achieve this relaxed approach to studies while, at the same time, helping students to remain focused on their work. According to Montessori, whenever both hand and brain work in unison, we find ourselves rested in our occupations. Such labor "does not retard study but on the contrary, helps to intensify it. . . . To devote oneself to an agreeable task is restful."[11]

Montessori used practical life exercises for younger children to engage both hand and brain, and for elementary children, the care of their environment. Adolescents are to have further responsibility for their environment including cooking, cleaning, sewing—even gardening and caring for outdoor animals where feasible. Activities are not only to be flexibly scheduled but there should be time for "observation of nature," which Montessori believed provides an "enrichment of the mind" from both a philosophical and scientific viewpoint.[12]

To facilitate contact with nature, Montessori envisioned a rural, although not isolated, setting for the *Erdkinder*. When Montessori died in 1952 the majority of the world's people still lived in farming communities. Today experiences in nature for the Montessori secondary level usually involve temporary outings in rural communities or parks: farming, hiking, camping, biking, and canoeing.

Montessori singled out farming activities for their benefits to adolescents. She believed that farming can help students develop a clearer understanding of the basis of human commerce and economic exchange and the complex issues which they represent for modern society. Further, they can give adolescents an experience with the scientific means whereby human beings have cooperated with nature in developing a kind of "supernature," such as hybrid plants, specialized breeding of animals, fertilizers, and farm machinery. The farm also affords the opportunity for adolescents to take part in the marketplace through a small store to sell produce. Montessori suggested that the harvest "constitutes an initiation to the fundamental social mechanism of production and exchange, the economic base on which society rests. This form of work then introduces the young person to the heart of social life by experience and study. A store presents the opportunity to learn about the social aspects of a successful business, as well as financial responsibilities of keeping inventory, accounting practices, sales, marketing, and government regulations.

Residential boarding schools were common in the European educational system during Montessori's lifetime; students often lived away from their families for a short trip or longer period. Montessori believed that any communal living situation should be regarded as an educational opportunity for young persons to experience independence within a working society. Their living quarters, whether temporary or of longer duration, should resemble "family houses." Married couples should live with the students in order to exercise "a moral and protective influence" over them. The students should manage all aspects of the houses, as well as overnight accommodations for visitors, thus acquiring "experience in all the various branches offered by the hotel enterprise, from the search for comfort to the social and material organization to the surveillance and control of finances." Because the youngest children keep their classroom and school environments orderly and enjoy doing so, Montessori believed that these same children as adolescents would not find it difficult to manage their own housekeeping.

Montessori considered that hands-on experiences with farming and the managing of a store or hotel would help adolescents "to consider work itself to be endowed with a greater importance than the kind of work to which one devotes oneself." Montessori believed that "all work is noble. The only ignoble thing is to live without working. It is essential to understand the value of work in all its forms, be they manual or intellectual. Practical experience will cause the adolescent to understand that the two forms are complementary and they are equally essential in a civilized existence."[13]

Experiences with commercial enterprises also have the possibility of giving adolescents a degree of financial independence. Montessori believed that this is an "essential reform" in an adolescent's education and that "their personalities will be enhanced by knowing that they can succeed in life by their own efforts and by their own merits." They will develop the independence "born from the ability to be sufficient to oneself and not from a vague liberty due to the benevolent and gratuitous help of adults."[14]

Montessori's emphasis on the child's goal of independence from the earliest years onward also suggests that at least limited experiences living away from home are beneficial to the adolescent. Such opportunities might help adolescents to view themselves less as children within a family and more as young persons in transition to adult membership in society and the full responsibilities which that membership implies.

The following anecdote provides an example of such an experience. The secondary-level teacher of a Chicago area Montesssori school arranged for a two-week outing for twenty thirteen- and fourteen-year-old students to a rural Wisconsin community. The small town of several thousand residents was a summer vacation area, so it was possible to rent a modest cabin. The young persons were entirely responsible for the shopping, supplies, and housekeeping during their two-week stay. Additional advantages of the area included a local branch of the University of Wisconsin and numerous historical sites, museums, and exhibits.

The cabin was adjacent to an organic-produce farm with a small herd of dairy cows. In addition to taking part in activities on this neighboring farm, plans were made for working visits to two other dairy farms, one with a herd of thirty cows and another with a herd of one hundred cows. Because of the different managing methods at the three farm locations, the children were exposed to varying approaches to milk production. For example, the larger farm used standard agricultural methods. The smaller farms operated on the Steiner method, a biodynamic approach in which the horns are left on the bulls, no chemicals or hormones are used, the animals are given names and treated as individuals by the owners. The farm owners using the biodynamic approach showed their financial analyses to the children, indicating that the lower daily milk production of the herds was balanced by longer life expectancies of the cows and savings on veterinarian bills due to the cows' better health.

At first, the adults on the farms appeared to see the children as a liability and an additional burden. They assigned the children only menial tasks, such as cleaning the barns and feeding the animals. Gradually, over the following days, the adults' attitude toward the children changed. Hired hands on the larger farm who had greeted the young persons with arms folded on the first day now were eager and happy to see them. One day, when the children returned after a day's absence, a hired hand greeted them by saying, "Where were you? We missed you guys." Thereafter, the children were shown how to clean the animals, sterilize their teats, and each day they attached and worked the milking machines. When several workers became sick one day, the farmer-owner told the young persons, "I don't know what I would have done without you today."

The close relationships and mutual admiration developed between the adults and the children were, in the teacher's opinion, one of the strongest benefits of the trip. Two girls, for example, got up voluntarily every day at 6:00 A.M. to go on rounds with one of the farm owners who was a woman veterinarian. The veterinarian arranged to show all the students a videotape of a calf being born. As it happened, the young persons also witnessed a live birth. Additionally, they were invited one day to see the castration of the young bulls at the larger farm. To the teacher's surprise, everyone opted to go. The thirteen- and fourteen-year-old boys helped hold the young bulls and asked questions of the veterinarian and teacher in later discussions. They were far more at ease in talking about the physiology of bulls than they had been in previous sex-education sessions. It was an opportunity for the teacher to start a discussion about the effects of testosterone in both animals and human beings who, unlike animals, are free to control their sexual behavior and must develop self-discipline, social mores, and responsible behavior. In this discussion, the students revealed an amazing naivete in regard to their own bodies, in spite of all the information that had been available to them in the past. They had confused vasectomy and castration, for example. This incident reinforced the teacher's conviction that learning and experience must go hand in hand; information alone is seldom sufficient.

Specific experiences also heightened the children's awareness of production and economic exchange. After observing the trucks come to pick up the milk at the farms for several days, the students asked where the milk would be sold and under what brand. Later when they bought this brand of milk in the store, they said with pride in their voices, "This might be 'our milk'!" The teacher planned to arrange work visits to a milk processing plant in the future.

In addition to farming activities, the students on this particular outing went to local botanical and zoological exhibits, several museums, and an historical site. They were polite on these visits but were not truly engaged by them. In contrast, the students were fascinated by an hour-long session in the geology laboratory of a University of Wisconsin professor. The cabin where the young persons were staying was close to a gravel pit where a number of them went exploring each afternoon. Because this gravel pit was at the edge of a glacial moraine, the students found a great variety of rocks and fossils there. They could not identify a number of them from the books which they had brought with them. The university professor did rock tests with the students and helped them make identifications. He was impressed with the level of their knowledge, stating that it was more advanced than many of his college freshmen. He was so pleased by their enthusiasm that he invited the students "to call me anytime." Subsequently, several of the students did so, continuing their relationship during the school year.

There was one more memorable experience during this particular outing. Local Native Americans were holding a powwow in the area, and one day the students were invited to come and observe the activities. At one point during the evening, the students were asked if they wanted to participate in the tribal dancing. The teacher had not prepared them for this unexpected invitation and was not certain how they would respond. To her surprise, the oldest boys, and the ones whom she was most concerned about taking part, were the first ones out into the dancing circle.

One of the unexpected outcomes of this two-week trip concerned the quality of interactions between parents and children upon the students' return. The parents had missed their children and began to set aside more time to be with them. Meanwhile, the students arranged an elegant dinner party for their parents.

They planned the menu, bought the ingredients, and cooked a gourmet meal including "chicken in parchment" as the main course. They served it with proper protocol in a candlelight setting complete with linen tableclothes, flowers, and formal place settings. Carrying out this elaborate event, they demonstrated their growing independence from their parents. At the same time, few communal events could have more clearly revealed the young person's continuing love and gratitude to their parents.

In evaluating the trip overall, the teacher felt that the close connections to adults involved in real work afforded the students the opportunity to take meaningful part in society as thirteen- and fourteen-year-olds and was of supreme value to young persons emerging into adulthood. At least for this two-week period, they were not reading or listening to others talk about the working world; they were directly engaged in it and learning from it for themselves. When taking students with her on morning rounds, the veterinarian had asked them, "What kind of work do you like best?" One student paused for a moment and then answered, "I've learned that it's not the work that you do but who you work with that counts."

The role of the secondary-level teacher in Montessori education is similar to that of the primary and elementary teacher; the secondary-level teacher is to serve as a link to the environment which is, in this case, the world at large. To do so effectively, the teacher's primary qualification is knowing and understanding adolescents. Acquiring such knowledge requires patience, faith, and skills of observation. Montessori particularly felt that adults have to take special care to show confidence in adolescents. They are in a sensitive stage of transition, no longer children and yet not adults. Montessori believed that "Respect for young people is essential. One must never treat adolescents as children. They are past that stage." They should not be given "the impression that they are not conscientious, that they are unable to discipline themselves. . . . It is of greater value to treat them as if their worth were superior to their real worth, than to minimize their merits and risk injury to their sense of personal dignity."[15]

All adults in Montessori education at any level are to be mature and responsible. However, Montessori singled out teachers of adolescents as requiring an unusual degree of self-discipline, character, and solid moral values. Montessori commented that adolescents have a tendency to rebel and question authority. In particular, they readily spot hypocrisy in their elders. This makes it imperative that the secondary-level teachers exercise a "severe discipline" in regard to their personal lives. By this means, they can "assure an ordered inner life and the unity of aims" within the *Erdkinder*.

The freedom of the adolescent, as of the child, is dependent upon the wisdom of adults in setting the proper limits on behavior. For the *Erdkinder*, this means that "the limits and rules must be observed by the entire institution." These rules, like those for the youngest children, "must be necessary and sufficient to maintain order and assure progress."[16]

When Montessori was asked about the unusual self-discipline of her students, she replied that they were disciplined because they were free. It is clear that Montessori's understanding of the primary role of limit-setting in the development of individual freedom accounted for the successful transference of Montessori's ideals into action in her educational environments. Montessori understood that freedom cannot be given by one individual to another; freedom can only be achieved through conquering one's self. In the words of the Hebrew proverb, "Who is a hero? One who conquers his own will."[17]

Montessori saw this conquering of one's self as the necessary means to human advancement and peace. Toward the end of her life, she wrote,

> human beings who have harnessed every kind of physical power, must now tame and tap their own inner power, become masters of themselves. . . . The fundamental freedom, the freedom of the individual is necessary for the evolution of the species for two reasons: one, it gives individuals infinite possibilities for growth and improvement and constitutes the starting point of the human being's complete development; two, it makes the formation of a society possible for freedom, the basis of human society.[18]

Montessori's understanding of the third plane of development as the one in which a sense of personal mission is shaped and young persons build the character and strength to enter working society, gives Montessori education at the secondary level great relevance in our modern world. High schools today prepare students for college studies. They allow for the development of the intellect. They do not concentrate to the same degree on guiding young persons to independence and the ability to adapt to social life. Indeed, regular education of the high-school level is geared toward egocentrism, not the good of society. Montessori provided not only a preparation for adolescents to take their place in working society as adults but she continually exposed them in their studies, from their earliest years, to those qualities in human beings which have led to the nobility of humanity.

Montessori believed that if young persons are given adequate help in their first three planes of formation, they will reach the final plane of development, the years from eighteen to twenty-four, ready to become "specialized explorers," beginning preparation for their personal careers. A career should have potential both for individual financial reward and for making a meaningful contribution to society. The belief that one's life work should have significance both personally and socially was grounded in Montessori's understanding of nature. She recognized that in the natural world each form of life, while pursuing its own survival through instinctual behavior, benefits the whole of creation. This realization prompted her to apply the same principle to human life. However, in human existence there is no instinctual guidance as to which role an individual should perform. As in all behaviors, human beings have a choice. The only choice they do not have if they wish to lead a fulfilling life, according to Montessori, is to make no choice at all.

Ideally, in Montessori education young adults are well-formed both individually and socially by the time they are eighteen years old. They have explored the organization of human society and its relationship to the natural world and are aware of the various careers which they might consider. In today's complex world of rapid and radical change, we know that a selection for one's life work, which is made before full adulthood is reached, is unlikely to define one's whole life. Certainly, Montessori who, in a much simpler historical period, changed careers herself in midlife, from medicine to education, would not find this a surprising outcome. An initial choice must be made by the young person with the recognition that other challenges and opportunities are likely to occur over his or her lifetime.

The psychological characteristics which Montessori identified for the fourth plane appear to support the young adult's choice and preparation for a career. This period is, first of all, one when the young person is again strong and relatively stable. In this respect, the psychological characteristics are similar to those of the second plane, the years from six to twelve. In the latter period, an integration of earlier formation results in the mature child. It is a stage characterized by energy and relative calm after a preceding six years of rapid change and turbulence. Now, in this last plane of adult formation, there is also an integration of earlier changes: this time, those of adolescence.

Because this is again a stage of relative peace after the tempestuous years of adolescence, there is a tendency for parents and society to ignore the true needs of young persons at this time. This is an error, both for individual young adults and for society as a whole. This is the adult's last opportunity to significantly influence young persons while they are yet in the formative stage. From this period on, any changes that are to be made must be accomplished by remedial means. Such means are costly in terms of time, energy, and financial resources. It is essential that adults respond to the great strength of young persons in these final years of adult formation by giving them the necessary attention and assistance.

According to Montessori, the help to be given in this period is to enable young persons "to become part of their society and to adapt to contemporary needs." This adaptation is to be achieved "by activity, by experience and by action" in the world itself. Young persons are to live and travel where they can study the problems and experience the cultural, business, scientific, and economic life of the modern world.

Montessori stated that "life is active and expansive and seeks creativity outside itself. Which is to say that to study is not to live, but to live is precisely what is most necessary in order to be able to study." In this final plane of human development, this means experiencing "Joy, the sensibility of one's value, feeling appreciated and loved by others, feeling useful and able to produce. These are factors of immense interest to the human spirit. The new university will have to draw its dignity from these factors and not only from culture."[19] To this end, Montessori believed that universities should help students find work experiences in the community. In this way, young persons could "find their own independence and social equilibrium" and "get a start toward economic independence." According to Montessori, "It would be a great advantage for students to achieve their financial independence during their university studies. Many young people are already teachers in private schools, journalists, artists, assistants at work in business, etc. Many are employed in laboratories or in diplomatic tasks. . . . If it takes them a few more years to complete their studies, it matters little, since their studies are never to finish."[20]

Montessori's own experience may have heightened her awareness of the young person's need for economic independence in the last period before assuming full adult responsibility. She lived at home with her mother and father during her university years, as was common for students in Europe at the time, but she earned scholarships and tutored students in order to pay her tuition, as her father disapproved of her unprecedented career choice.

Helping students to experience various career options, however, is not to take the place of intellectual studies as the major mission of the university. Montessori believed that "education should continue throughout life. . . . The very function of the university is teaching to study. The diploma is nothing more than proof that one knows how to . . . acquire culture by oneself . . . that one has been shown the way to do scientific research. . . . A man or woman who studies at the university knows that it is necessary to study all one's life or study will lose all its value."[21]

The role of the prepared adult during the final plane of formation is to serve as a link to the whole of society. This role as "link to the environment" is a key in this last stage of the educational process as it was at its beginning. In some ways, it is more important since society supplants the family in influence with the young person. Indeed, for many students, college is their first experience in living away from their families.

At the fourth plane, the linking process is almost entirely a mentoring experience, rather than the direct connecting to the environment of the earlier stages. The young person has already developed the capacities necessary for successful interaction with the environment: independence, discipline, motivation, and social responsibility. What are needed in this last stage are wise adult counsel, encouragement, and support. In small liberal arts colleges, no additional research is necessary to demonstrate these needs of young college students: Admissions officers are aware that the single most important reason given for college re-enrollment is a personal connection to a professor.

According to Montessori, one of the goals of the university professor, as mentor, is to guide the students to an appreciation of the need for continued study and thought throughout life.

Such study should not only occur as an independent activity but in association with others. This emphasis on communication with others in thinking and learning, and the synergy that results, is a continuation of the natural tendency of children from their elementary years onward.

Montessori noted this tendency to collaboration early in the child's life when freedom and responsibility are given:

> We have seen how association among children occurs spontaneously, all by itself, for purposes of thinking and understanding. It seems that true comprehension goes hand in hand with discussion, with criticism and with the approval of others. It is necessary that the pleasure of knowing be immediately communicated to someone else. . . . Study and thought call for association just as does manual work. . . . Spontaneous collaboration is a truly revealing manifestation. Association brings new strength with it. It stimulates new energies. *Human nature needs society as much for thought as for action.*[22]

It is in the area of career choice that adults carry the heaviest responsibility to persons in the fourth plane. As the last counselor to them while they are still in the formative stage, he or she, whether university professor or other significant adult, can aid young persons in the development of what many adults fail to experience in life after schooling is over, a place in the world that has meaning beyond one's own existence.

The freedom that was given to young persons from the beginning of their education in the Young Children's Community and extended gradually with their growing self-discipline in each succeeding educational environment, now reaches its fullest expression. If all has gone well, freedom in this final stage of formation should be complete.

Montessori recognized that it would not be possible for universities and colleges to adopt a plan of study that combined advanced intellectual study with extensive student participation in the society at large unless young persons were prepared for it in their earlier formative stages. She found that when universities sought to develop "their own plan of study, they find the students insufficiently prepared to follow it; it is the same in the secondary school with reference to the elementary school. And everybody feels the burdensome obstacle that is the lack of preparation of the personality." Instead, it is "necessary to establish coordination between all phases from childhood to maturity, from the nursery to the university. Because a human being— even though he or she passes through interdependent phases—is nonetheless a single entity. The preceding level prepares for what follows by laying the foundation."[23]

By following the path of education that Montessori suggests with its emphasis from the beginning on the development of the human being in each successive plane, young persons can reach the last stage of their formation prepared to become "specialized explorers." They will be ready to choose and prepare for at least a first career in their adult lives while, at the same time, continuing their intellectual studies. Most important of all, they will have confidence in their own abilities to learn. By this means, they will be enabled to expand and renew their knowledge throughout their lives.

10

△ △ △

MONTESSORI:
PRESENT AND FUTURE

Thirty years ago, almost no parent that I talked to had heard of Montessori education. I remember one young mother even thinking that Montessori was the name of a new brand of spaghetti.

Over the next ten to twenty years, I began to come in contact with an increasing number of young parents who knew the Montessori method was a form of education for young children. Invariably, however, they had significant misconceptions as to its focus. "Oh, yes, isn't that the system where the children are encouraged to run wild and do whatever they like?" a parent might respond. Or, conversely, another might say, "That's the European education that is so strict, isn't it? Where the children aren't allowed to talk or play with each other but have to do everything the exact way that the teacher shows them?"

Today the name "Montessori" is not only recognized as a form of education by the majority of young parents that I meet, but a great number of them have some understanding that it seeks to combine encouragement of initiative and independence in learning with development of self-discipline and responsible social behavior. This gradual public awareness has followed from the establishment of over three thousand Montessori schools affiliated with a national or international Montessori organization and as many as one to two thousand others which are not so aligned. This significant and continuing growth of Montessori schools has taken two different directions—first in the private sector and more recently in the public sector.

In the private sector, Montessori schools began with primary programs for children ages three to six years old. Beginning in the mid-1980s, a dramatic increase occurred in the number of these schools extending to the elementary levels for children ages six through twelve years old. By the mid-1990s, this expansion reached to the middle school and junior high school with programs added for twelve to fifteen year olds. At the same time, an extension downward to include children younger than three years old occurred with the establishment of parent-infant programs and young children's or toddler communities.

The evolution in the public sector has had a different starting point but has followed the same goal of extending Montessori education to all age groups. Since the public-school system historically has begun with children five or over, the first public Montessori programs were begun at kindergarten and first-grade levels and were gradually expanded to include the remainder of the elementary years. These public school programs have been instituted in one of two ways: either as "magnet" schools or through the establishment of charter schools with the nation's first charter school being a Montessori school in Minnesota. (Charter schools are established under state charter laws that allow states to fund a limited number of schools that are contracted by local school districts but which are operated independently, either by their teachers, parents, or community organizations. Magnet schools are established and funded by local school districts to create special programs which, by their uniqueness, attract geographically, economically, and racially diverse populations, particularly in inner cities.)

From the beginning Montessori magnet schools have been enthusiastically supported by parents. Year after year, Montessori magnet schools across the country have maintained long wait lists, ranging in the number of children hoping for a space from the hundreds to over a thousand. One magnet specialist says, "There is no doubt about the power of Montessori magnets to attract. They have consistently sustained excited teachers, involved parents, and a wide cross-section of children. They are the first schools to meet their enrollment."

Regardless of the administrative structure under which these public Montessori programs have been established—charter or magnet—their developmental paths are similar. Montessori public schools have begun as elementary programs for children ages six to twelve years old. Over time, the demand for offering Montessori education to children under school age, as well as continuing with children of middle-school age, has led to an expansion of classes to include these age groups. Because public schools typically do not have funds for the establishment of programs for children under five years old, Montessori advocates apply for Head Start grants for this purpose.

In order to familiarize Head Start officials and others in the educational establishment with Montessori education, an historic re-creation of a demonstration primary classroom which Montessori established in San Francisco at the 1915 Panama

Pacific Exposition was organized for the 1995 annual convention of the National Association for the Education of Young Children (NAEYC). Twenty-five thousand educators from public and private schools and child-care centers attended this conference held at the World Congress Center in Atlanta, Georgia.

The model classroom was developed by the Montessori Institute of Atlanta[1] and primary children and teachers from three different local Montessori schools participated, each coming to class there for one day of the three-day event. The classroom was enclosed on three sides with partitions and open at one end to bleachers which could accommodate up to two hundred spectators. The children, ages three to six years, paid little attention either to these visitors or to the Montessori teacher trainer as she answered the observers' questions and explained the ongoing activities of the children.

Many early childhood educators indicated that this was their first opportunity to witness Montessori children at work. They mentioned that seeing the children in action dispelled many of the negative stereotypes they had earlier believed about Montessori. One Head Start administrator said, "I was always under the false impression that Montessori environments were lacking in language stimulation, but seeing this classroom has changed my idea completely." Other administrators and public-school leaders from across the country expressed their enthusiasm for Montessori education after witnessing this classroom in action.

The movement of Montessori into the mainstream of public and private education is an opportunity to reach the ultimate goal of accessibility for all children. There is a negative side to this laudable aim, however, of which parents should be aware. As Montessori methods are disseminated to a larger audience, it may become rarer to find authentic Montessori schools. Montessori represents a revolutionary approach to children's education. When the educational establishment embraces ideas that are foreign to its experience, misunderstandings and compromises can occur. If as a result of the latter, Montessori concepts are not implemented properly, the children will not reach the expected levels of development. Those involved will become discouraged and disillusioned. This could happen in Montessori education, as it has in other reform movements in education. A decade from now "Montessori" might be a generic term, much as the label "kindergarten" in American education today, referring primarily to an extension of schooling below the elementary grades. Montessori education's most practical asset, and the one which distinguishes it from other educational reforms of recent years would be lost: namely, the details of a working plan for aiding the development of young children, which has proven successful in primary and elementary classroom settings around the world.

Several factors are necessary if this unfortunate outcome is to be avoided. Teachers of all Montessori programs must be thoroughly trained in Montessori theory and practice. To achieve this result, good training courses must be available in all areas of the country, both for new teachers and for experienced teachers who are new to Montessori education. Subsequently, these trained teachers must have the tools necessary for implementing quality Montessori education. This means that they must be given the resources to establish quality "prepared environments": classrooms which are based upon the principles of order, beauty, and simplicity and which contain the Montessori materials for the appropriate age levels.

Additionally, parent involvement is important. Because it

takes time for parents to understand Montessori concepts, which depart from older methods of education, the first step in establishing Montessori schools should be the establishment of parent education programs. When this is done initially, many potential problems are averted.

All three of these criteria—teacher training, classroom preparation, and parent programs—involve start-up costs for Montessori schools. However, it is important to realize that the operational expenses of Montessori classrooms are significantly lower than those of customary classrooms. This is because regular school programs rely on textbooks, workbooks, and other materials limited in scope and rapidly outdated. They must be continuously replaced at enormous expense. Further, regular education is subject to constant changes and fads. "Old math" to "new math" and back to "old math" is a recent example. Additional costs accompany each one of these curriculum changes, not only in materials, but in teacher retraining as well.

Montessori materials, on the other hand, representing basic concepts, are applicable to children from every background and country. They have stood the test of time for almost a century on six continents and are not subject to drastic change. They are built, therefore, to last: well designed, expertly crafted, and durable. As such, they represent a capital, versus a continuing, expense.

Because Montessori education is not influenced by educational fads, funds are also saved in the area of in-service teacher training. Although ongoing education of teachers is always necessary to maintain the highest standards of classroom practice, future training for Montessori teachers builds upon the base established in their initial training course. This base focuses on the development of children and their universal needs, regardless of their individual situations. There is always more to learn in these areas. However, nothing must be unlearned. The expense of ongoing training and workshops for Montessori teachers is thereby minimized.

Many Montessori organizations are working to safeguard the integrity of Montessori education as it continues its rapid expansion in the United States. While maintaining their individual identities and standards, these groups have formed an umbrella organization, the Montessori Accreditation Council for Teacher Education (MACTE).[2] The goal of this organization is to guarantee the supply of well-trained Montessori teachers from all backgrounds. For example, one of MACTE's projects is to have certified Montessori courses included in the existing government-assistance programs allocated for teacher training.

The frontier for Montessori education is the availability of quality Montessori schools for all children, regardless of their economic background. Today's graduates of Montessori programs will help to determine whether this frontier is reached. If these students continue to make strong records in their new schools, whether going on to upper elementary grades, junior or senior high schools or, in some cases, directly to college, the impetus for parents and educators to embrace Montessori education will increase.

To date, studies of Montessori children, including those from a low socioeconomic status, show that graduates have benefited significantly from Montessori programs at both the preschool and elementary levels. They have scored higher on nationally standardized tests than their non-Montessori peers. Equally important, they have been rated higher in characteristics important to school success, such as the ability to use basic skills, follow directions, complete work on time, listen attentively, ask provocative questions, and adapt to new situations.[3]

Anecdotal evidence also corroborates the ease of adjustment for Montessori students to new educational settings at every level. Students from my own school, Forest Bluff, for example, have adjusted quickly to new school routines and expectations. In response to the novel experience of heavy homework assignments at a new middle school, the parents of one graduate reported that their son did his homework each night without prodding and that he is receiving top marks as a student in all advanced classes. He defines the difference between his two schools matter-of-factly: "In Montessori you work in school. In my new school you work at home." Other Forest Bluff students have thrived in new situations as well entering new schools at the elementary or high school levels. They have received top grades, participated in extracurricular programs, won prizes, and adjusted easily to social relationships. Most important, they have not lost their enthusiasm for learning nor their trust in their teachers to serve as reliable and supportive mentors. As to college placement, the first two Forest Bluff graduates who began their Montessori education at age three are currently students at Stanford and Northwestern universities.

There is one more factor to consider in the final outcome of Montessori education's future in the United States. To my mind, it is the most important one of all. It is the attitude of Montessori graduates toward their own schooling. Montessori education purports to help young persons develop a lifelong love of learning, the ability to work effectively in teams to solve problems, and individual strength of character, courage, and confidence to face life's challenges. If Montessori graduates perceive that they have achieved these goals, they will not be satisfied with any other form of education for their own children. Sometimes when I have a discouraging day in the classroom or I feel disheartened with the state of the society and the world, I remember this and my enthusiasm for life and for teaching returns.

One day not long ago, I asked my eleven-year-old grand-daughter, Margaret, who has been a Montessori student since she was two years old, the perennial adult-to-child question: "Did you have a good day at school today?" "It was not good," she answered with a shy smile and sparkling eyes. "It was *great*!" I believe that there is one fundamental reason for a young person of any age having this positive reaction to a day in school. He or she is being given, on a daily basis, the help and support needed in each stage of development, year after year, from the beginning of his or her schooling to its ending. Montessori education follows just such an approach. It focuses on each child as one continuously developing person from birth to early adulthood. The needs of each stage of self-formation are met. Montessori education is a cohesive system, following the logical path of coordinating one phase of education with the next so that all phases, taken together, present one harmonious whole.

Historically, this has not been true of regular education where little coordination has occurred between levels: preschool to elementary, junior high school to senior high school, college to graduate school. Fortunately, educators today, including leaders in the field of higher education, are calling for a recognition of this fundamental flaw and a realization that it is here, at its foundation, that the restructuring of American education must take place.[4]

Montessori had the vision to encompass the whole of human development in her approach to education. By working directly with children in the first two stages of life, from their birth to six years old and from six through twelve years old, observing and experimenting on a daily basis, she developed "working drawings" to implement an educational plan for these two periods of childhood. We have only her "architectural design" for the planes of emerging adulthood: twelve to eighteen years and eighteen to twenty-four years. The fleshing out of this overall design into daily practice remains a pioneering project for today's educators. In the meantime, the framework of this plan serves as the backdrop against which Montessori education for preschool and elementary children is best understood.

Today's technological revolution has made the world's information accessible to anyone who can master the computer and access the Internet. It is no longer practical to cut up information into digestible pieces and parcel it out to students in a formal school or college setting, whether by lecture or textbook, and to consider such a process to be an education for a lifetime. Educators can serve as mentors to stimulate the learning process for the student, but only an intensive, individually initiated pursuit of knowledge over the entire span of life will gain each one of us the education necessary for the twenty-first century.

Montessori did not consider the child as a blank to be written upon—an historical concept that is as inconsistent with contemporary understanding of human development as Newtonian physics is dated as a basis for human organization and business management. For her, the child is a distinct, unique being with an infinite capacity and enthusiasm for learning. Montessori's overriding goal for the young adult was the development of a passion and capacity for lifelong learning. No purpose for education could be more pertinent to our world today and tomorrow.

APPENDIX

A STUDENT'S REFLECTIONS
Rebecca Makkai

Every parent of a child in a Montessori school invariably asks how the child will fare when he or she eventually enters a regular school system or goes on to university. Rebecca Makkai entered high school upon graduating from the Forest Bluff School at the age of thirteen. In her own words, written a few weeks before her high school graduation, she reflects on her Montessori education and its preparation for life. She plans to continue her studies at university this fall with the intention of pursuing a writing career.—Ed.

One of the images that most clearly sticks in my head of my early years at Montessori is the bucket-on-the string experiment. I remember peeking around the door-frame of my Junior Level One class and watching the

"Older Children." They had taken a small tin pail filled with water and tied a thin rope to the handle. And now, to my astonishment, they picked up the rope and started swinging the bucket in the air, in huge, sweeping circles. As I was about to run and tell on them for doing such a terrible thing, I noticed something even more amazing—something which challenged my newfound perception that there was no such thing as magic: *The water was staying in that bucket.* A few years later, I tried the same experiment myself, and learned that the only magic there had been something called centrifugal force; gravity had not been defied, but merely obeyed. The magic was in the nature of the water.

Standing by when I learned how to perform this "magic" myself was the teacher—she had gathered a group of us for a presentation—an event for which we all held the greatest respect. It was now, we knew, that we would be able to understand what the Big Kids already knew about the world, and such amazing things as flying buckets of water.

These presentations were, indeed, just that—the world was being presented to us, as was our place in that world. On my first day of school, when I was five, the teacher announced that everything in the classroom had a name. She challenged us to find an object that did not; we couldn't. We then began to learn the names of things outside the classroom—the types of trees on the lawn, and the types of leaves on them—the parts of an apple—the parts of a lizard—the states in the country—the countries of the world. We learned also our responsibility to and role in that world. We saw the tiny silhouette representing mankind at the end of the long sheet representing time. We learned that this was us. We saw that the potted plants and the groundhogs in the cage in the corner needed us as caretakers. We learned that we were that, also. We saw that there were pictures to be painted and plays to be written and worms to be dissected—and so we became artists and writers and scientists.

Since the world had been presented to us, we, in turn, presented ourselves to the world. In Montessori I was allowed to delve into venues of creativity, to explore interests, however fleeting, and to develop passions. And, amazingly, my teachers were as receptive to my presentations as I had been to theirs. They sat patiently through long skits and even longer reports; they listened intently as we raised our hands to tell stories, even when they knew they weren't true.

We were encouraged wholeheartedly to create and experiment and explore; I found myself with more freedom in the fourth grade than I would have in my senior year of high school.

I figured out early on, as most of us did, that the Montessori teachers had handed us their unconditional trust. We were free to do what we chose, from picking what we would work on to moving freely around the classroom. I can't imagine how different my education would have been had I been denied the basic rights to talk and move around—had I, like my friends at other schools, viewed my teachers as wardens, rather than friends.

In a world where "Give 'em an inch and they'll take a mile" seems to be the golden rule, this trust is refreshing. The Montessori teachers gave us a mile, and because they respected us enough to do so, we respected them enough to run that mile as hard as we could. This momentum carried me through high school as well. The respect with which I had been instilled remained, as self respect, and I therefore pushed myself to excel—to exceed the goals which had been set for me.

One of the first presentations we received in science was about the natures of solids, liquids, and gasses. While solids stay constant and gasses are without form, we were told that liquids flow freely, expanding and moving to fit the shape of their container. Children are liquid. They shape themselves to fit the form of the container into which they are placed. Where they are free to go, they go; what they are free to do, they do. And when they are accorded this freedom, they feel no need to push its boundaries.

Children thrive on trust. When allowed to walk to town, they do just that; when allowed to paint a picture, they do just that; when allowed to work for hours mastering intransitive verbs, they do just that—and gladly. I am forever indebted to my teachers for their amazing "presentation" of absolute trust to a young child.

They had enough faith to swing the bucket, because they knew that it was in the very nature of the water to remain right there.

NOTES

PREFACE

1. The international headquarters for the Association Montessori Internationale, the organization founded by Maria Montessori in 1929 for the continuation of educational research and training of teachers, is headquartered in Amsterdam, The Netherlands (161 Koninginneweg. 1075 CN). The U. S. Branch Office is at 170 W. Schofield, Rochester, New York 14617, (716) 544-6709.

CHAPTER 1

1. Maria Montessori, *The Four Planes of Education*, p. 1.

2. Antonio R. Damasio, *Descartes' Error*, p. 107. Also see remainder of book for pertinent information on the human being's self-construction and brain development.

CHAPTER 2

1. E. M. Standing, *Maria Montessori, Her Life and Work*, p. 112.

2. See Restak, Richard M., *The Modular Brain*.

3. E. M. Standing, *Maria Montessori, Her Life and Work*, pp. 206–207.

4. *Ibid.*, p. 208.

5. Maria Montessori, *The Child, Society, and the World*, pp. 60; 65.

6. *Ibid.*, p. 73.

7. *Ibid.*, p. 23.

8. E. M. Standing, *Maria Montessori, Her Life and Work*, p. 345.

9. Mario Montessori, Jr., *Education for Human Development*, pp. 31–41.

10. E. M. Standing, *Maria Montessori, Her Life and Work*, p. 74.

CHAPTER 3

1. Maria Montessori, *To Educate the Human Potential*, p. 7.

2. Maria Montessori, *The Four Planes of Education*, p. 5.

3. Maria Montessori, *The Child, Society, and the World*, p. 27.

4. Maria Montessori, *From Childhood to Adolescence*, p. 23.

5. *Ibid.*, p. 12.

6. *Ibid.*, p. 6.

7. *Ibid.*, p. 37.

8. Maria Montessori, *To Educate the Human Potential*, p. 14.

CHAPTER 4

1. Maria Montessori, *To Educate the Human Potential*, p. 8.

2. *Ibid.*, pp. 5–6.

3. *Ibid.*, p. 9.

4. *Ibid.*, p. 52.

5. $(a + b)^2 = a^2 + 2ab + b^2$

6. Maria Montessori, *From Childhood to Adolescence*, p. 36.

7. *Ibid.*, p. 134.

8. Unpublished lecture by Margaret Stephenson, recorded from AMI Elementary Training Course, Montessori Institute of Milwaukee.

CHAPTER 5

1. Maria Montessori, *To Educate the Human Potential*, p. 1.

2. Peter Gebhardt-Seele, *The Computer and The Child*.

3. Maria Montessori, *From Childhood to Adolescence*, pp. 76–82.

4. Maria Montessori, *To Educate the Human Potential*, p. 52.

CHAPTER 6

1. Maria Montessori, *To Educate the Human Potential*, p. 6.

2. An event occurring in Europe in the late 1930s may have helped Montessori to be keenly conscious of the connection between moral values and independent thought in education. Because the fascist state of Mussolini was intent upon indoctrinating children with specific

views, all Montessori schools were ordered closed by the government in 1937. A similar order by the Nazi regime was given soon afterward in Germany. Montessori schools with their emphasis on freedom from indoctrination were the only schools in either country to be so selected.

3. Maria Montessori, *From Childhood to Adolescence*, p. 12.

4. *Ibid.*, p. 63.

5. *Ibid.*, p. 25.

6. Maria Montessori, *To Educate the Human Potential*, pp. 95–96.

CHAPTER 7

1. Maria Montessori, *From Childhood to Adolescence*, p. 10.

CHAPTER 8

1. The earthquake that occurred in Kobe, Japan, in January, 1995.

2. Marsilia Palocci is an international Montessori teacher and trainer and a member of the Pedagogical Committee of the Association Montessori Internationale. She is trained at three Montessori levels, birth to three by Costa Gnochi, three to six by Maria Montessori, and six to twelve by Mario Montessori, Jr. She has over thirty years of experience as a classroom teacher.

3. Trevor Cairns, *The Coming of Civilization* (Cambridge: Cambridge University Press, 1986) and *People Become Civilized* (Minneapolis: Lerner Publishing Company, 1974). Charles Higham, *The Earliest Farmers and the First Cities* (Minneapolis: Lerner Publishing Company, 1977).

4. The content and purpose of the individual meetings with each child is outlined in Chapter 7, pp. 101-2.

CHAPTER 9

1. Notes from these lectures were published in synopsis form as three appendices to a book on Montessori elementary education published in French in 1948. This book was translated into English as *From Childhood to Adolescence*.

2. Maria Montessori, *Four Planes of Education*, pp. 7–8.

3. Maria Montessori, *From Childhood to Adolescence*, pp. 98; 111.

4. See William Hobson, *The Chemistry of Consciousness: How the Brain Changes Its Mind*, for a contemporary commentary on this view.

5. Maria Montessori, *Four Planes of Education*, p. 8.

6. The experience of such organizations as Outward Bound and NOLS (National Outdoor Leadership School) substantiates this insight.

7. Maria Montessori, *From Childhood to Adolescence*, p. 114.

8. From a presentation by John Long made at the NAMTA conference in Portland, Oregon, November 10, 1994.

9. Maria Montessori, *From Childhood to Adolescence*, p. 124.

10. *Ibid.*, pp. 119–125.

11. *Ibid.*, p. 104.

12. *Ibid.*, p. 106.

13. *Ibid.*, pp. 106–109.

14. *Ibid.*, pp. 102–103.

15. *Ibid.*, p. 115.

16. *Ibid.*

17. Pirke Avot.

18. Maria Montessori, unpublished lecture.

19. Maria Montessori, *From Childhood to Adolescence*, pp. 133–135.

20. *Ibid.*, p. 138.

21. *Ibid.*

22. *Ibid.*, p. *135*.

23. *Ibid.*, pp. 130–132.

CHAPTER 10

1. Montessori Institute of Atlanta, 2355 Virginia Place N.E., Atlanta, Georgia 30305.

2. MACTE, Joy Turner, Director, 17583 Oak Tree, Fountain Valley, California 92708.

3. David Kahn, "Montessori in the Public Schools," Montessori Public School Consortium, 11424 Bellflower Road N.E., Cleveland, Ohio 44106.

4. William Brock, ed., *The American Imperative: Higher Expectations of Higher Education*, pp. 19–20.

BIBLIOGRAPHY

Brock, William, ed. *An American Imperative: Higher Expectations in Higher Education.* Racine, Wisc.: The Johnson Foundation, 1993.

Brooks, Jacqueline and Martin. *In Search of Understanding: The Case for the Constructivist Classroom.* Association for Supervision of Curriculum Development, 1993.

Damasio, Antonio R. *Descartes' Error.* New York: C. P. Putnam's Sons, 1994.

Damon, William. *Greater Expectations: Overcoming the Culture of Indulgence in America's Homes and Schools.* New York: The Free Press, 1995.

Gatto, John Taylor. *Dumbing Us Down.* Philadelphia: New Society Publishers, 1992.

Hobson, M. D., J. Allan. *The Chemistry of Consciousness.* Boston: Little, Brown and Company, 1994.

Lillard, Paula Polk. *Montessori: A Modern Approach.* New York: Schocken Books, 1972.

———. *Children Learning.* New York: Schocken Books, 1987.

Long, John. "Survey of Montessori Adolescent Programs: Interpretive Commentary," *NAMTA Journal Special Report* (July, 1994).

Montessori, Maria. *To Educate the Human Potential.* Thiruvanmiyur, Madras: Kalashetra Publications, 1948.

———. *Education and Peace.* New York: Henry Regnery Company, 1972.

———. *The Formation of Man.* Thiruvanmiyur, Madras: Kalashetra Publications, 1955.

———. *From Childhood to Adolescence.* New York: Schocken Books, 1973.

———. *The Child, Society, and the World.* Oxford: Clio Press, 1989.

———. *The Four Planes of Education.* Amsterdam, Netherlands: Association Montessori Internationale, 1971.

Montessori, Mario Jr. *Education for Human Development.* New York: Schocken Books, 1976.

NAMTA Journal. "Montessori Frameworks for Adolescence," Vol. XVIII, No. 3 (Summer, 1993).

Restak, Richard M. *The Modular Brain.* New York: Macmillan Publishing Company, 1994.

Gebhardt-Seele, Peter. *The Computer and the Child, A Montessori Approach.* Rockville, Md.: Computer Science Press, 1985.

Standing, E. M. *Maria Montessori, Her Life and Work.* London: Hollis Carter, 1957.

INDEX

New from Schocken in Summer 2003
Montessori from the Start
The Child at Home, from Birth to Age Three

From two of the country's leading Montessori educators, **Paula Polk Lillard and her daughter Lynn Lillard Jessen**, the first book to focus on Montessori methods for infants and children at home.

What can parents do to help their youngest children in their task of self-formation? How does the Montessori method of hands-on learning and self-discovery relate to the youngest infants? This authoritative and accessible book answers these and many other questions.

Brimming with anecdote and encouragement, and written in a clear, engaging style, *Montessori from the Start* is a practical and useful guide to raising calm, competent, and confident children.

ISBN: 0-8052-1112-8 • $13.00 paperback (Can. $20.00)

Other Montessori titles available from Schocken by Paula Polk Lillard:
Montessori Today
0-8052-1061-X • $12.00 paperback (Can. $16.95)
Montessori in the Classroom
0-8052-1087-3 • $14.00 paperback (Can. $19.50)
Montessori: A Modern Approach
0-8052-0920-4 • $12.00 paperback (Can. $16.95)
by Maria Montessori:
Dr. Montessori's Own Handbook
0-8052-0921-2 • $12.00 paperback (Can. $18.00)
The Montessori Method
0-8052-0922-0 • $14.00 paperback (Can. $17.50)
www.schocken.com